CW00536687

WIGTON
THROUGH TIME
Trevor Grahamslaw

AMBERLEY PUBLISHING

First published 2010

Amberley Publishing Plc
Cirencester Road, Chalford,
Stroud, Gloucestershire, GL6 8PE

www.amberley-books.com

Copyright © Trevor Grahamslaw, 2010

The right of Trevor Grahamslaw to be identified
as the Author of this work has been asserted in
accordance with the Copyrights, Designs and
Patents Act 1988.

ISBN 978 1 84868 806 3

All rights reserved. No part of this book may be
reprinted or reproduced or utilised in any form
or by any electronic, mechanical or other means,
now known or hereafter invented, including
photocopying and recording, or in any information
storage or retrieval system, without the permission
in writing from the Publishers.

British Library Cataloguing in Publication Data.
A catalogue record for this book is available from
the British Library.

Typeset in 9.5pt on 12pt Celeste.
Typesetting by Amberley Publishing.
Printed in the UK.

Introduction

I was aged ten when my family moved to Wigton in 1969. My first impression was of a small compact town, with family run shops lining the streets and everyone seemingly related to each other. On market days and Saturdays the town became alive as the streets surrounding the Market Place bustled with shoppers, patiently queuing at the grocer's, baker's and butcher's, drifting in and out conversations as the events of the previous few days were turned over. Entertainment was sport, clubs, concerts and The Baths, with evening bike races and games played in the jumble of alleyways and lanes leading to the near empty Water Street car park. For adults there was the pub or club, dances, sport and church.

After leaving school my interest in documentary photography developed and I began to take and collect Wigton pictures. Soon the antiquity of this old town became clear. The older properties part build from Roman stone robbed from the ruined fort at Old Carlisle, the mediaeval pattern of the streets, the dwellings and industry established near water courses and the town shape, forming a rough cross centered on the Market Place.

This book has been designed to trace a route through these streets, following this cross-shaped pattern. Commencing at Old Brackenlands, only yards from the remains of the Roman settlement, then travelling north to the former common land at Southend, transformed by the Bank's family of Highmoor into a gentleman's estate. A detour is taken to Longthwaite, Lowmoor and the Baths Path, where Wigton's townscape can clearly be seen resembling its adopted name 'The Throstles Nest', nestling in the landcape.

From Southend to the magnificent Georgian terraces of High Street, past the Cornmarket and St Mary's Church to the very heart of the town the Market Place. Once the site of an actual market cross, the Pump and Lamp and now the exquisite George Moore Memorial Fountain. Built in the classical style; this treasured monument is dedicated with genuine feeling to George Moore's wife Eliza.

East of the Market Place is the commercial King Street. Then Church Street and Water Street, once packed with poor back-to-back houses and industrial warehouses. Today most of these properties have gone, replaced by the Water Street car park. Further east is Market Hill and East End, formerly the haunt of weavers who worked hard and drank hard, often gambling their wages backing fighting cockerels at the Market Hill cockpit. This former tough area is yet another car park surrounded by modernised housing.

North to Bog Road, where an open sewer once carried factory waste into the River Wiza. Renamed Station Road it remains an industrial area, dominated by the Innovia Films factory. Beyond the railway is Station Hill with its fine mansions, today almost severed from Wigton by the road bypass.

West you pass Brookfield, the Park and Barton Laws, which has witnessed so many grand occasions from Circus Big Tops to the annual crowning of the Carnival Queen. Before returning via West Street to the Market Place.

Comparing these old and new photographs, you can sense that Wigton is becoming more cosmopolitan. New housing has sprung up at the town's four corners and accents from outside Cumbria are audible on the street, as new people attracted by Wigton's rural aspect and outstanding schools have moved into this cosy town on the Solway Plain. Yet Wigton is maintaining its identity and has recently been compared by Melvyn Bragg, the town's most famous son to a quotation by the poet and artist William Blake, 'To see the world in a grain of sand', all human life is here, and continues to flourish in this small market town, as these pictures prove.

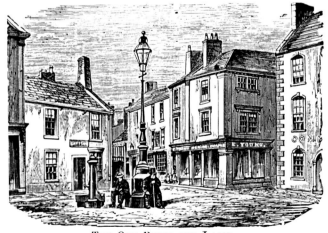

THE OLD PUMP AND LAMP

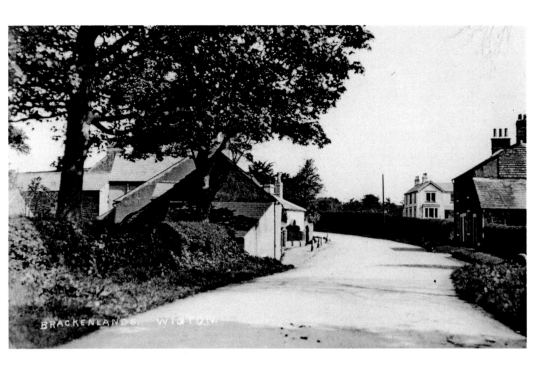

Old Brackenlands

A charming photograph of Old Brackenlands situated at the southern entry into Wigton. Left is Brocklebank Cottage with the appropriately named Townend Cottage together with Ivy Cottage forming the terrace on the right. South Bank House clearly viewed in the earlier picture is now obscured by trees and has been divided into two residencies, South Bank and Greengarth.

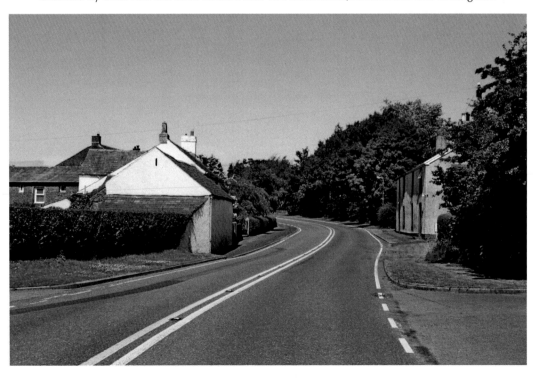

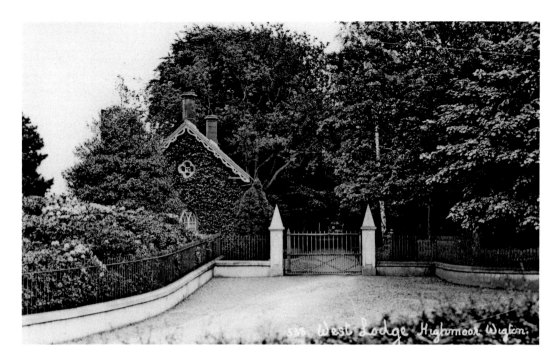

West Lodge

West Lodge, Southend c. 1900s. Through the gate was a elegant tree lined avenue stretching for a quarter of a mile to Highmoor mansion. When Highmoor estate was auctioned in 1909 the avenue was sold separately, being developed in the 1930s when the trees were felled and houses build on the avenue's southern side. The avenue road remained separating the houses from their gardens on the northern side. Today the Lodge is a private residence with the gateway pillars and perimeter wall surviving.

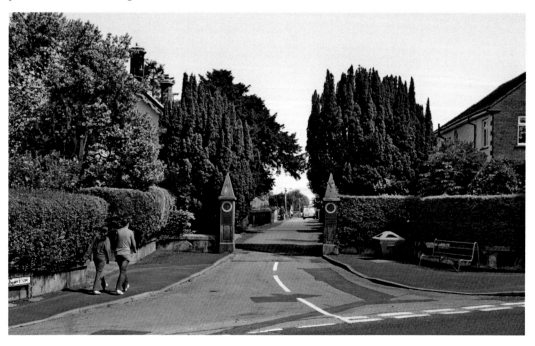

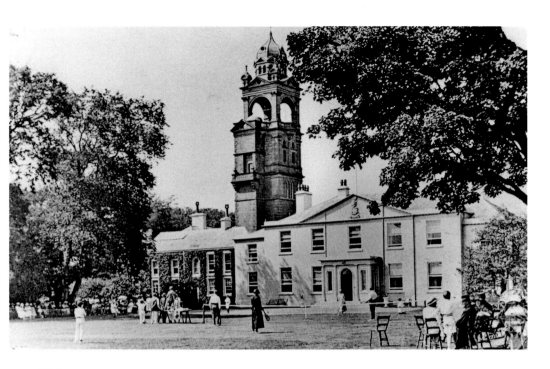

Highmoor

Highmoor mansion built in 1810 by Joseph Hodgson a textile manufacturer. Later owned by William Banks and then his sons Henry and Edwin, who enlarged the estate and added an Italian style tower. Equipped with chiming clock, large bell and a carrillion of bells which played tunes during the week and hymns on Sunday the tower dominated Wigton visually and audibly. In 1909 the then owner Edwin Banks was declared bankrupt and the house sold. This 1920s photograph of a Highmoor garden party was taken when the Hon. Gilbert de St Croix owned the house. In 1934 Highmoor mansion was converted into flats whilst private housing has subsequently encircled the house.

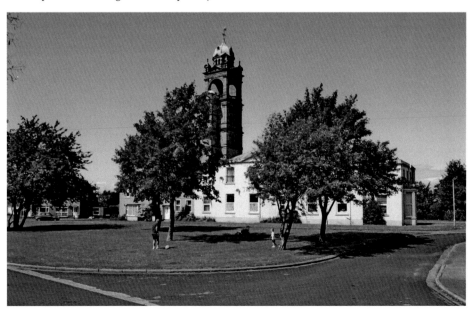

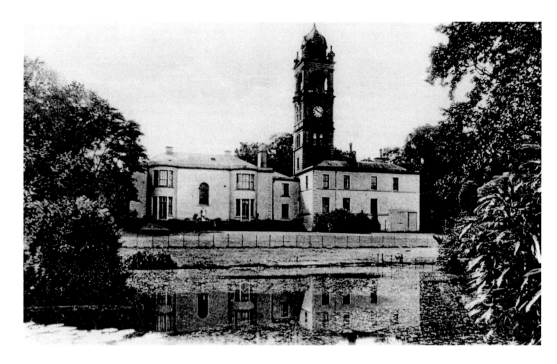

Highmoor Pond

The Highmoor estate was full of surprises, the parkland was landscaped with exotic trees, deer and llama roamed the park, and the pond pictured here was home to flamingoes. By the 1970s the pond had silted up, hidden in a wilderness of vegetation. So in the 1990s local residents Tom and Anne Crozier assisted by Ian Green and other helpers voluntarily drained the pond, repaired the sandstone banks and have returned the pond to its former glory, and a welcome home for waterfowl.

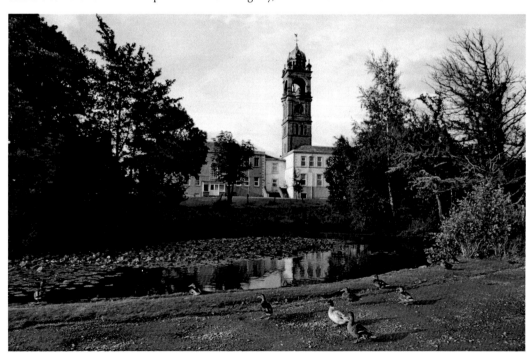

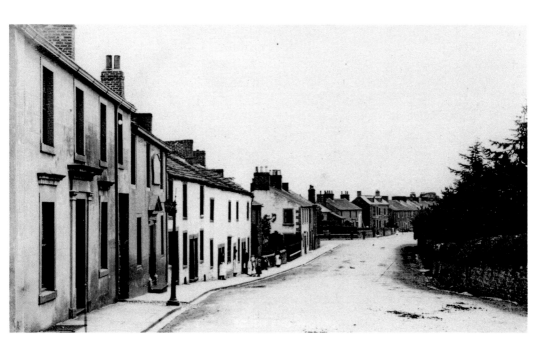

Southend

Past West Lodge, Southend proceeds downhill as pictured here. The second property on the left with the inn board is the Greyhound. Once frequented by weavers, ragmen and potters (who would park their caravans in the Greyhound yard during the winter), the pub was also a haunt of John Woodcock Graves author of the hunting song 'D'ye Ken John Peel'. Right behind the hedge was Mount Pleasant a former market garden. The site is now a housing estate named Mount Pleasant Gardens, with the entrance just before the petrol station on the second picture.

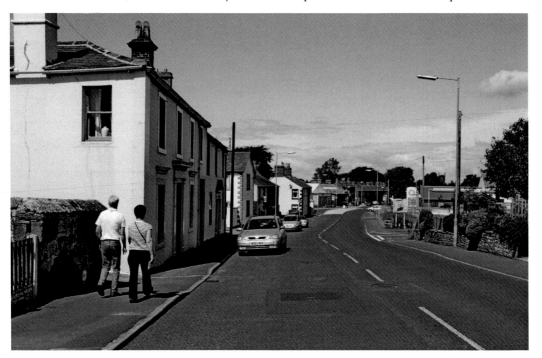

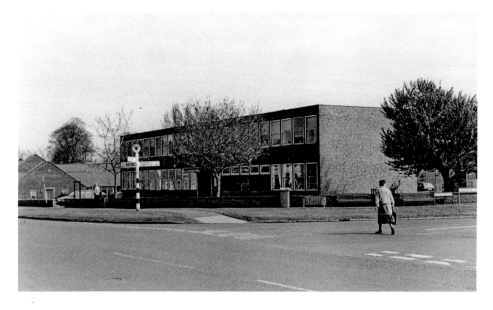

Council Offices

Wigton Council Offices was built in 1965 to replace the former Wigton Urban District Council headquarters sited in three antiquated George Street cottages. The Council Offices building estimate was £30,000 which spiralled to £58,000 despite substantial building cuts. Never loved the Council Offices building was considered extravagant and the architecture undistinguished by most Wigtonians, although Pevsner's *Buildings of England* described the building as "a straightforward honest job without gimmicks".

Demolished in 2004, the building was replaced by Wigton Medical Centre seen here. Right of the Medical Centre positioned on the site of a former pinfold, is the perimeter wall of one of Andy Goldsworthy's Cumbrian sheepfold sculptures. The original pinfold would have been used as a pound for collecting stray animals from Highmoor and Lowmoor common land before the moor was enclosed in 1810.

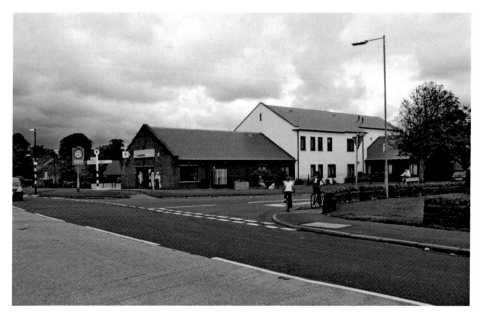

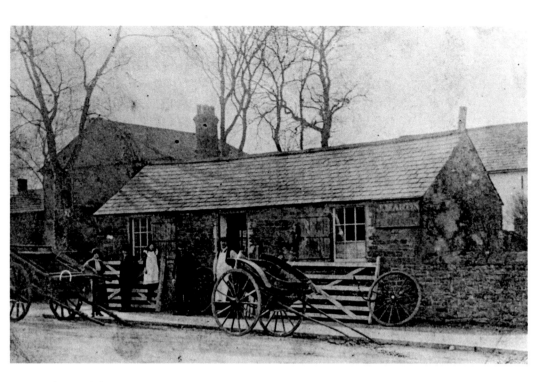

Jack Martin's

Jack Martin joiner and wheelwright in the white apron stands beside a cart, outside his workshop in 1912. Situated on the crossroads of Southend, Lowmoor Road and Longthwaite Road, Jack's workshop was idealy located on the southern outskirts of Wigton. Converted into the 'Mini Market' and run by David and Isabella Pearson, the premises were rebuilt in the 1970s. The second picture shows the current owner Chris Bell with the shop van at the new Mini Market, a newsagent and grocer it is the only remaining shop on Southend, serving newly built estates and the nearby Nelson Thomlinson and Infant School.

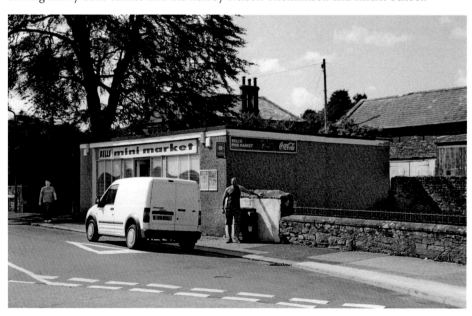

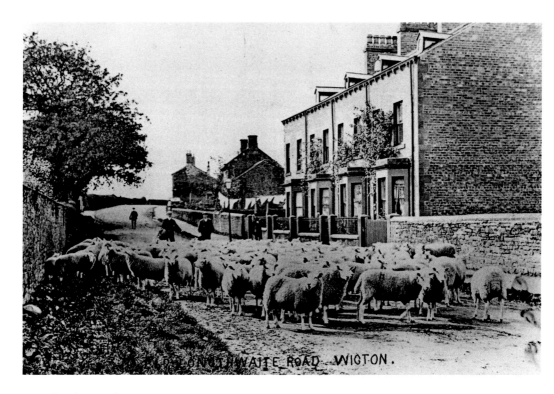

Longthwaite Road

Washing hangs out to dry beside South Terrace, as sheep ready for market are driven down Longthwaite Road for sale at Hope's Auction Company Ltd in Church Street. Once a peaceful rural road, Longthwaite Road is now a busy thoroughfare to the new housing estates of Longthwaite Crescent, Primrose Bank and Springfields situated just over the hill on the second picture.

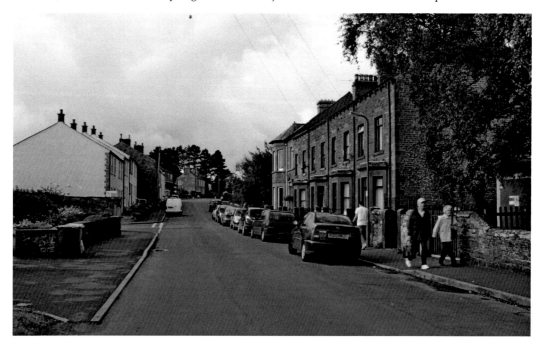

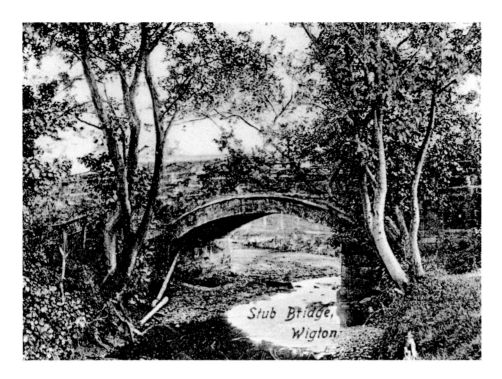

Stubb Bridge

Right on the edge of Wigton Parish Boundary just off Longthwaite Road, Stubb Bridge marks the start one of Wigton's most useful footpaths, following the River Wiza through Barton Laws to High Wiza Bridge on West Road. In summer the bridge is almost hidden by vegetation, and in winter only glimpsed through branches. The recent photograph proves how popular the footpath remains, here enjoyed by dog walkers in the January snow.

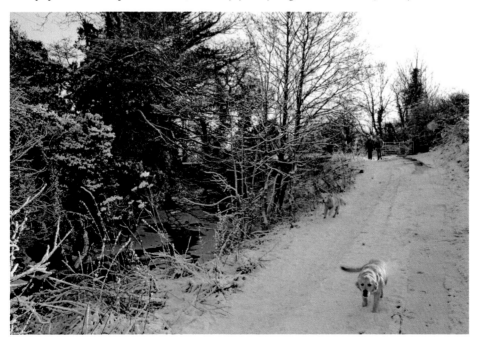

13

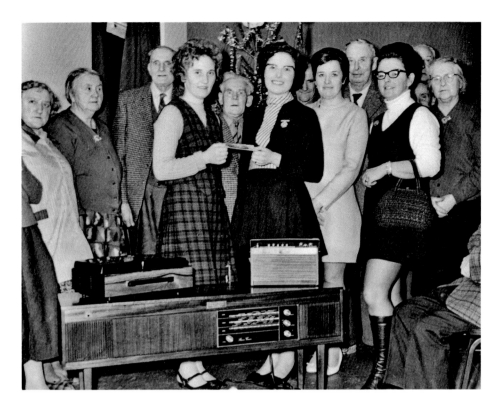

Inglewood

Officer in Charge Pat Grahamslaw surrounded by some of the residents of Inglewood care home, accepts a state of the art music centre on behalf of Inglewood from Wigton Ladies' Circle, shortly after the home had opened in 1969. A purpose built care home Inglewood celebrated its fortieth birthday in 2009 and has only had two managers (Mr Edkins being the current officer). The bottom picture shows Inglewood on Lowmoor Road.

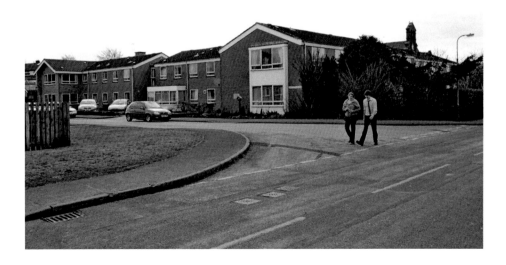

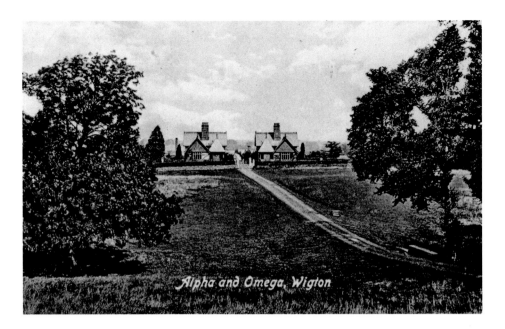

Alpha and Omega, Wigton

Alpha and Omega

This fine cobbled path connected Highmoor estate farm and stables with the estate workers cottages Alpha and Omega on Lowmoor Road. Built in the style of Swiss chalets the two cottages were situated just outside the two miles of iron fencing (still standing today) erected in 1878 to encircle the Highmoor estate. The path permitted access to the farm and parkland and would once have resounded to the noise of Edwin Banks galloping racehorses. A keen sportsman Edwin Banks stabled, 'Old Joe' the 1886 Grand National winner and 'Mosshawk' a prize winner at the 1887 Royal Show of Champions. Today the farm is derelict, the stables demolished and the parkland either built on or returned to fields. But the path remains as a popular short cut to town and school.

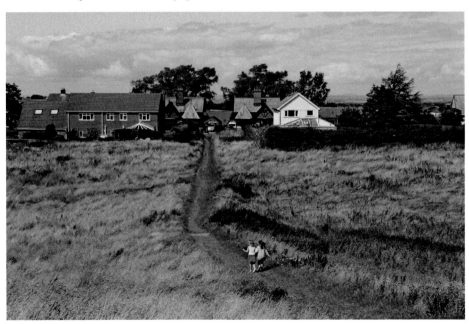

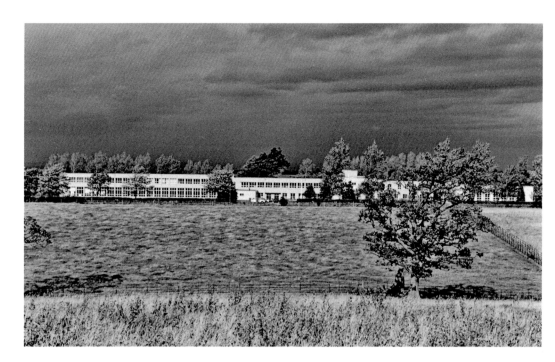

Middle School

Menacing rain clouds advance on a sunlit Middle School in 1990. Built in 1949 in compliance with the 1944 Education Act, Wigton Secondary School was a technical school for pupils who failed the eleven plus examination. In 1969 the school was amalagamated with the Nelson Thomlinson grammar school as comprehensive education was introduced and renamed the Middle School. The superior facilities were always at the grammar school site, which continued to expand and improve. In 1996 the Middle School was sold to McAlpine builders who demolished the building and replaced it with the housing estate Scholars Green, seen here from Highmoor.

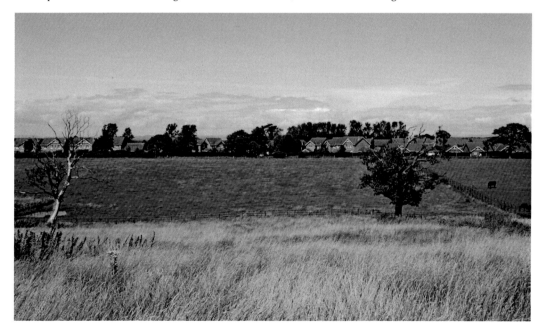

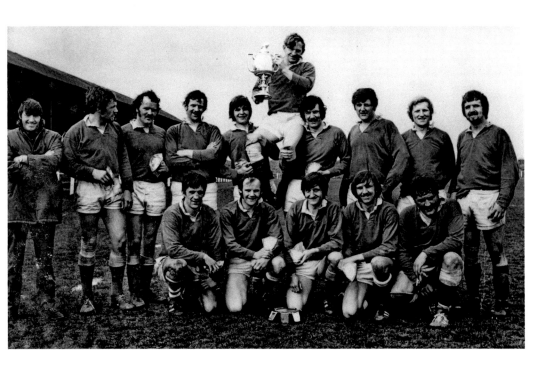

Wigton RUFC

Keith Warwick captain of Wigton RUFC holds aloft the Cumberland Cup in 1978. Wigton's first rugby club, Highmoor Rangers played at Highmoor Park in 1882. Folding in 1886 they were superseded by Wigton Excelsior who played until 1889. Finally in 1906 Wigton RUFC formed to play on the Kings Arms field, then Highmoor, and finally Barton Laws before purchasing land for their own pitch at Lowmoor Road in 1967 for £5000. Success quickly followed with five Cumberland Cup triumphs in the 1970s. Since then the club has developed into a major sports complex, fielding three senior teams, colts teams and sharing facilities with cricket, squash and hockey sides, whilst a £425,000 all weather pitch opened in 2009. The 2009-10 season first team pictured below have recently been promoted as champions of the North Lancashire and Cumbria League.

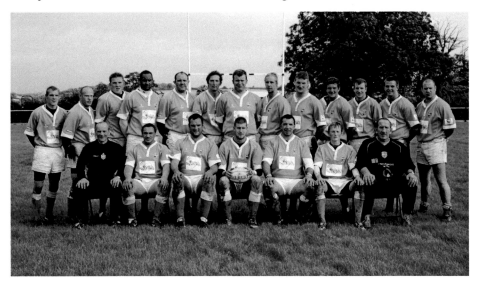

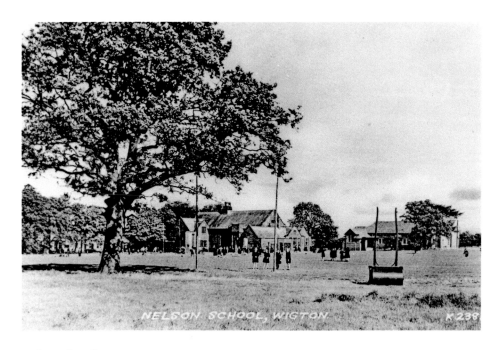

Nelson Thomlinson

Joseph Nelson made a fortune from textile manufacturing. A bachelor, he left his money to a charitable trust. In 1896 Floshfield House, here glimpsed behind trees on the left of the old picture, and grounds was bought for a boys school. The house was converted into the headmaster's residence and boarding accommodation for pupils. Whilst the Nelson School (behind the rugby posts) was built in 1898. This picture was taken after 1952 when the Nelson Boys and Thomlinson Girls schools had joined to create the Nelson Thomlinson School, as girls are standing in the foreground. The second picture shows part of the twenty-first century Nelson Thomlinson which specialises in maths and computer studies.

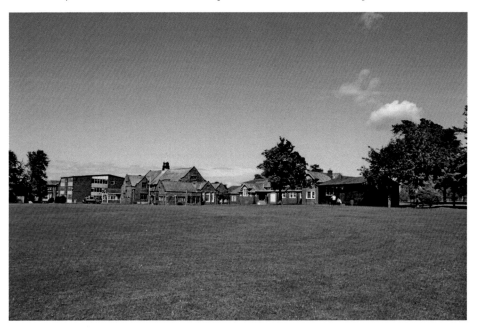

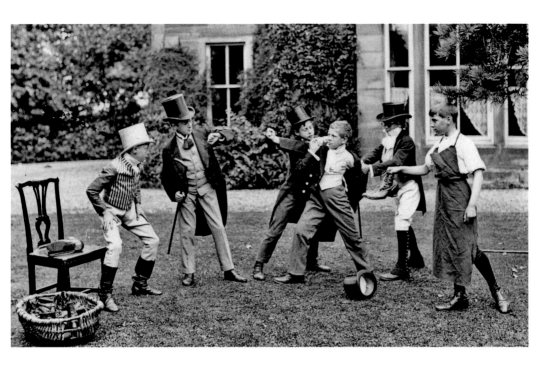

School Fête

Rated academically outstanding in a recent Ofsted inspection, there is still a place for tradition and fun at the Nelson Thomlinson. This early picture beside Floshfield House, shows Nelson school boys rehearsing a scene from Charles Dickens novel *Pickwick Papers* for the 1911 speech day. Whilst a 1991 school fête organised by the Nelson Thomlinson Parent Teachers Association features stalls and donkey rides to raise school funds.

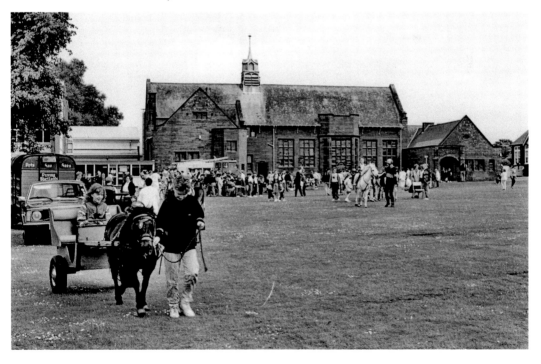

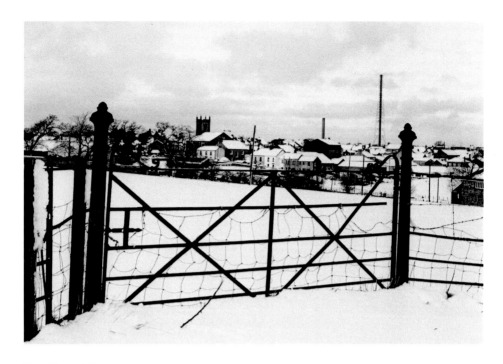

The Throstle's Nest

Apart from the western end, all roads go downhill into Wigton which lies in a hollow or nest hence Wigton's nickname The Throstle's Nest. This striking 1980s winter scene from the Bath's path shows the heart of the town nestling in the landscape. St Mary's tower and the factory chimneys dominate the skyline, with Hopes Auction buildings on the left and the Baths right. In the centre lies Laurel Terrace and the United Reformed Church. The later image taken after the January snowfall shows few changes, apart from Inovia Films new factory block left of St Mary's.

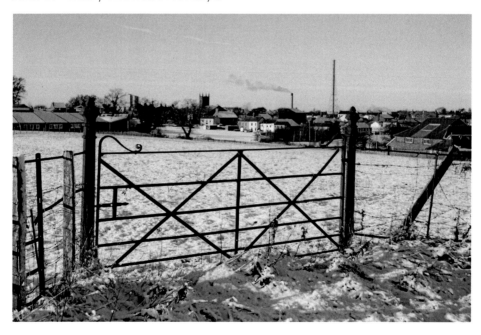

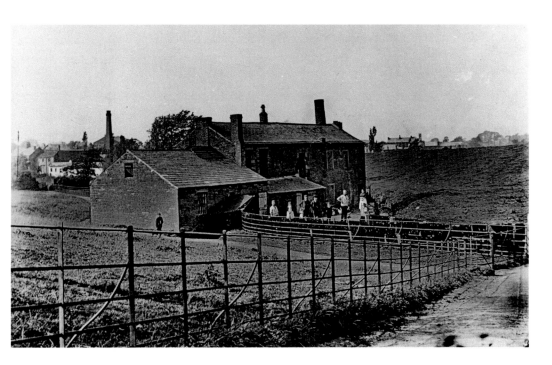

Little Mill

It is hard to believe today but in the nineteenth century Speet Gill was one of Wigton's most important energy sources providing power to run breweries, tanneries, dye houses and mills including Wigton Little Mill here. Built in 1783 Little Mill was used for grinding corn when Edwin Banks bought it in 1879. In 1901 he demolished the mill, built the Baths, then gifted it to Wigton Urban Council. The Council declined this philanthropic offer, fearing upkeep costs and instead agreed to lease the Baths for one shilling a year. With Edwin Bank's bankruptcy the Council had to buy the Baths which is currently managed by Cumbria County Council. The second view shows the baths, with the gently flowing Speet Gill (out of sight) behind the tree on the right.

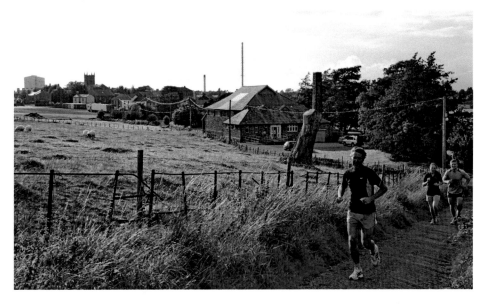

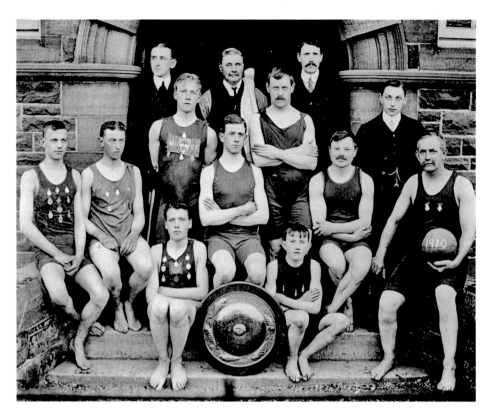

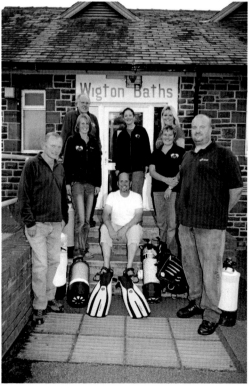

Water Polo

The 1910 Wigton Water Polo team proudly show off the Cumberland Shield in Wigton Baths entrance. The team went on to be unbeaten for a further eleven years, being rewarded in 1921 with a prestigious friendly against the touring Swedish Olympic team. The Swedes proved too strong defeating Wigton by six goals to one ending their unbeaten run. 1921 was also the year when the Baths Commitee allowed mixed bathing, but only on condition that proper costumes were worn and the Bath's manager and his wife were present poolside. It would be interesting to know there opinion on the mixed sub aqua Solway Divers club pictured here who use the Baths for training.

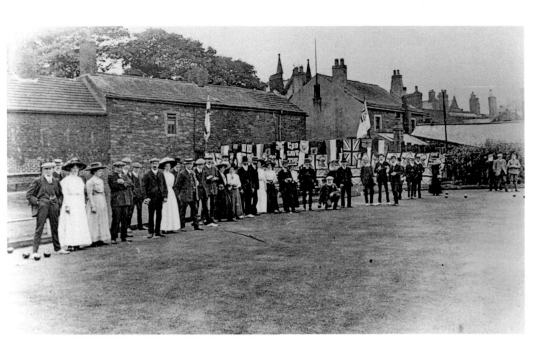

Throstle's Nest Bowling Club

Flags and posters celebrating the 1910 coronation of George IV, are proudly displayed at the Throstle's Nest Bowling Club green situated behind the Highland Laddie Inn. In 1961 the need for a connecting road between High Street and Water Street resulted in the bowling green's closure, and demolition of the properties on the left. The second picture shows the Stocksman Restaurant car park and road (once the bowling green), the Thomlinson Junior School (left), the Methodist Church (centre) and the Highland Laddie now a private residence (painted white). The flag of St George continues to fly above the Wigton Memorial Garden opened in 2009 in remembrance of the fallen from two World Wars.

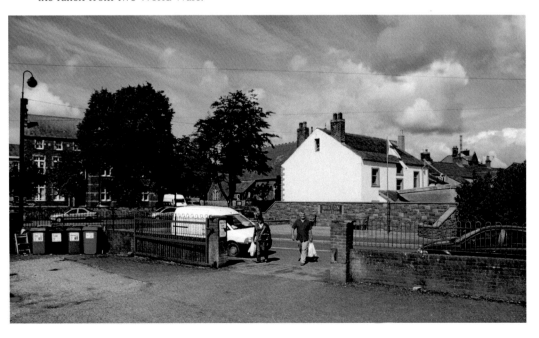

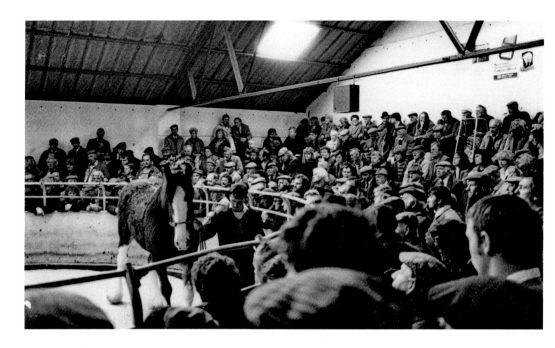

Hopes Auction Company

Farmers and dealers pack the sale ring for Hopes Auction Company's 1987 horse sale. Hopes was founded in 1897 by Jonathan Hope who opened his mart in Church Street. Today the Mart is on High Street and has twice weekly sales of livestock, together with a thriving estate agency, hotel and antiques sales business, but the glamour event is the horse sale. Held since time immemorial, customers come from all over the country to buy and sell. The bottom picture shows a 2009 sale with Bruce Walton auctioneer.

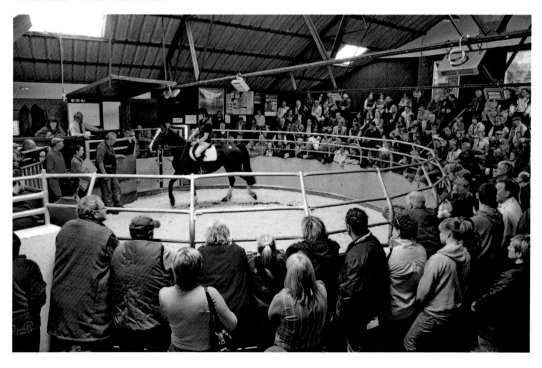

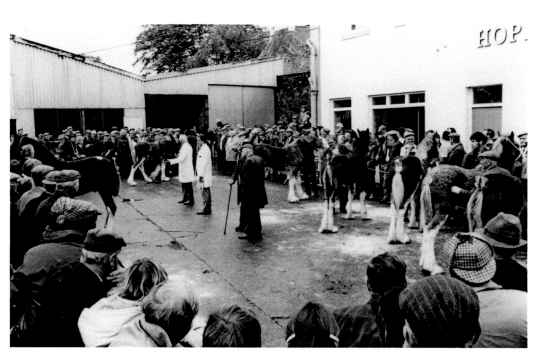

Auction at Hopes

Another 1987 photograph with auctioneers Joe Benson and Andrew Wright selling horses outside. Still one of the largest horse sales in the north of England, Wigton's horse sale is no longer three days long, but remains popular as old acquaintances are renewed. Today farm implements and even boat sales are often held outside the ring, but like all Hopes events many farmers attend to catch up on the 'crack' (gossip) before making a deal. This snap from 2009 shows auctioneer David Bowman and Betty Graham selling farm machinery in Hopes car park beside Laurel Terrace.

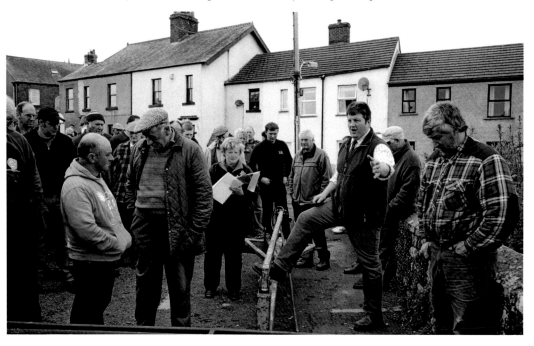

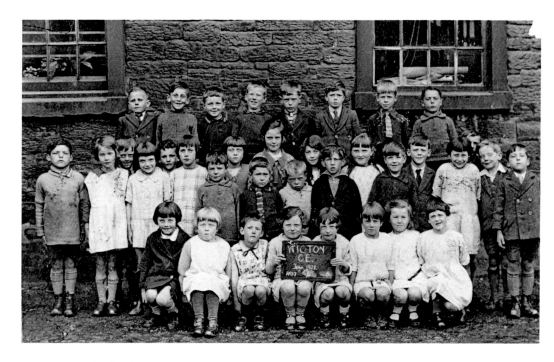

National School

The two girls in the foreground balance a blackboard reading 'Wigton C.E. June 1928' on this mixed classes picture at the Church of England National School. Built in 1829 the school was segregated with boys taught downstairs and girls upstairs, there was even separate playgrounds. Condemned in 1910 the school was still used until 1968 when the pupils were moved to the Thomlinson Junior School at Westmorland House (the former Thomlinson girls school) and segregation ended. The National School building, pictured here from the Nelson Thomlinson School entrance, became Tynedale Farm Services agricultural warehouse, and is currently being converted into Charlotte Court a housing development.

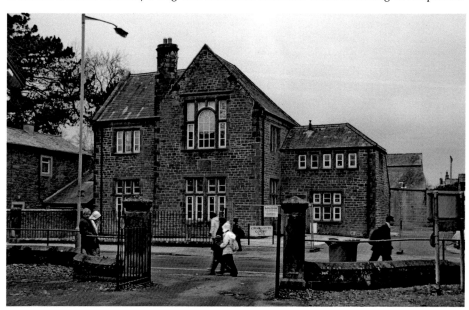

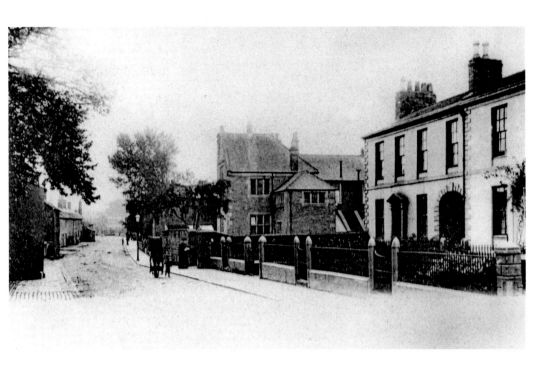

Clifton Terrace

A comparison of these two pictures taken a hundred years apart shows many interesting changes. Clifton House on the left and the former Toll Cottage remain, but the row of weavers' cottages further up the street were demolished on the instruction of the governors of the Nelson Thomlinson School who consided them structurally unsafe and 'the abode of disreputable people'. Across the road is the National School, then the former garden of Clifton House, now occupied by a 1930s property The Flosh. Finally right is the fine Georgian period Clifton Terrace little altered apart from an addition of Victorian bay windows to the right-sided property Kumara.

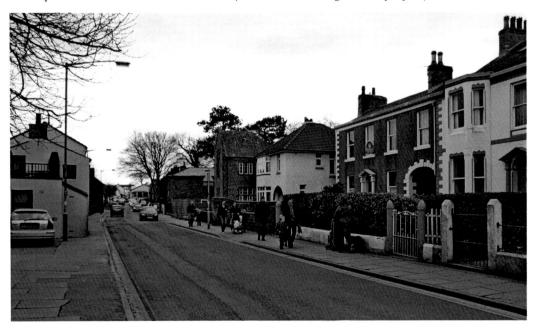

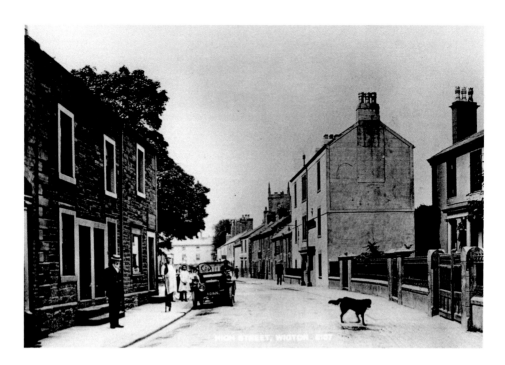

Cheesy Brough

Joseph Brough known as 'Cheesy' to the National School pupils stands outside his shop at 54 High Street wearing a grocer's apron, the premises now trading as Stitch & Print retails clothing. Beside Joseph is one of the first cars in Wigton dating from 1914. Across the road painted blue and white on the modern picture is the former Highland Laddie Inn now a private residence whilst beside it is the sandstone wall of the Wigton Memorial Garden. The connecting properties up to the three-storey building at No 87 have been pulled down.

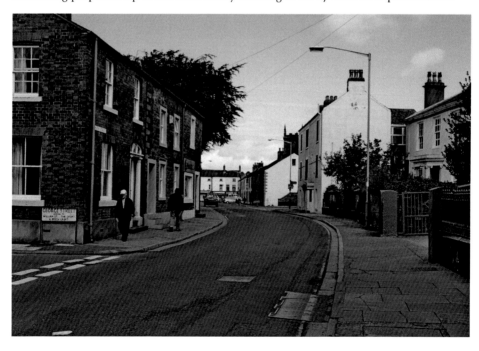

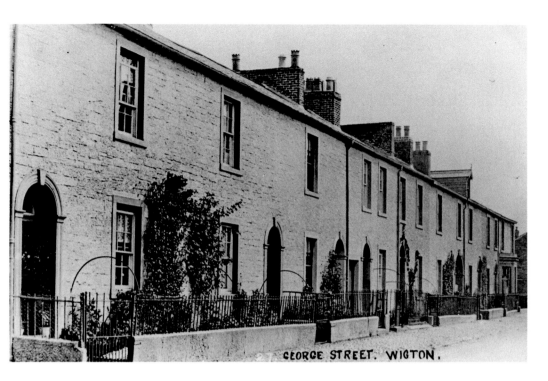

GEORGE STREET. WIGTON.

George Street

These fine Georgian town houses gracing George Street date from 1826. Once the residences of clergymen and businessmen, many of the houses were surprisingly rented by weavers and hatters in the 1850s. This was the boom time for Wigton's textile industry, as George Street would have resounded to the clicking shuttle, box and treadle of handlooms, and the industrious workings from Joseph Sheffield's hat manufactory in neighbouring William Street. Today George Street is purely residential and one of Wigton's most attractive streets.

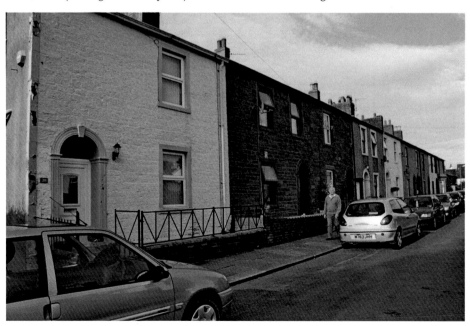

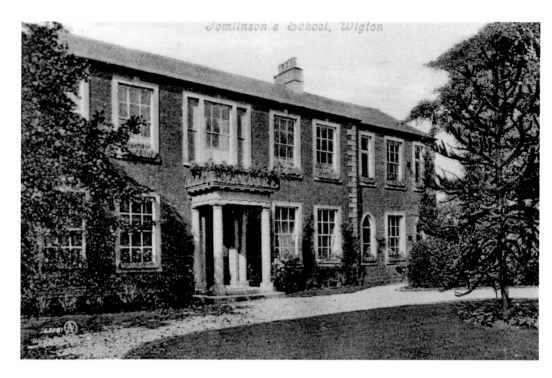

Thomlinson School

Thomlinson Girls School opened in 1899, named after John and Robert Thomlinson whose donation had enabled Wigton's first grammar school on Market Hill to open. The red brick extension shown on the modern picture dates from 1908, with the earliest part of the school Westmorland House on the left. It was built on the site of Flosh House by John Westmorland a wealthy merchant who made his fortune managing Jamaican plantations. Westmorland House was later owned by Isaac Pattinson the textile manufacturer before becoming a school. Today it is Wigton Junior School.

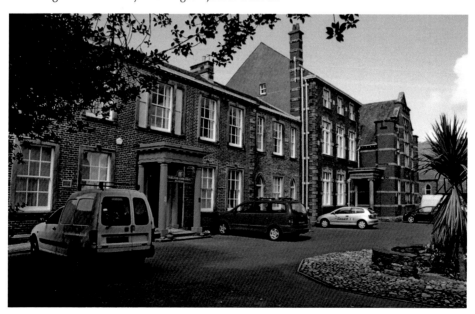

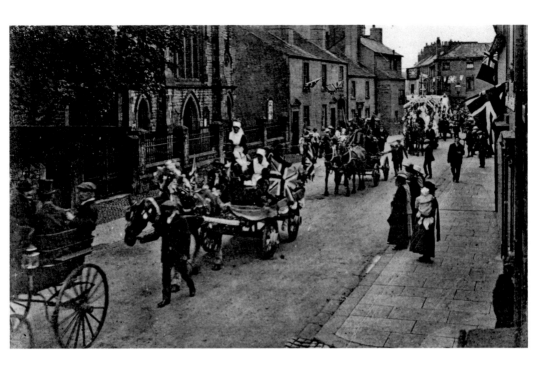

Parades

Wigton people have always enjoyed parades and rarely need an excuse to dress up and march down the street. This picture shows a peace parade passing down High Street to celebrate the end of the First World War. Whilst the second photograph is of the 2009 Carnival Queen Abigail Thomason waving as her innovative royal float, constructed to resemble the Moore Memorial Fountain passes Wigton Methodist Church.

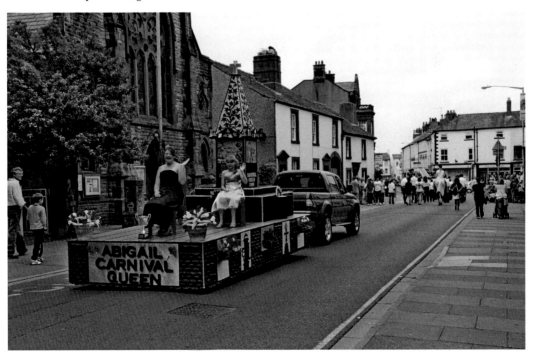

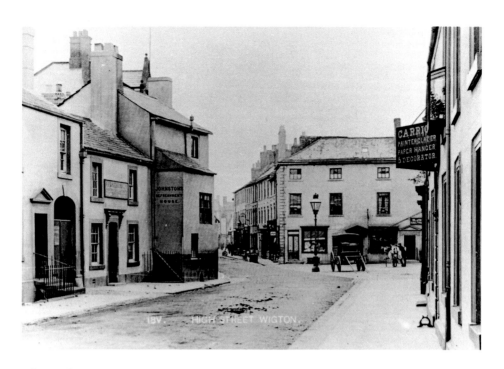

Johnston's Tearooms

Compare these two views of High Street looking into the Cornmarket. On the older picture left, is Armstong's Restaurant now a private house, then Johnston's Tearooms. Owned by Joseph and Rebecca Johnston the tearoom was also a grocery and game dealer and a firm favourite with market day farmers. Pulled down in 1981 to make way for a road into Croft Court housing estate its demolition has opened up a view of the Kildare Hotel. Beside a taxi on the Cornmarket is the Lamp, since removed and now in Water Street, whilst right Robert Carrick painter, glazier and decorator's shop is now a private residence.

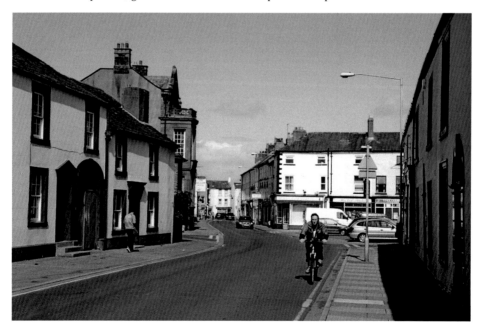

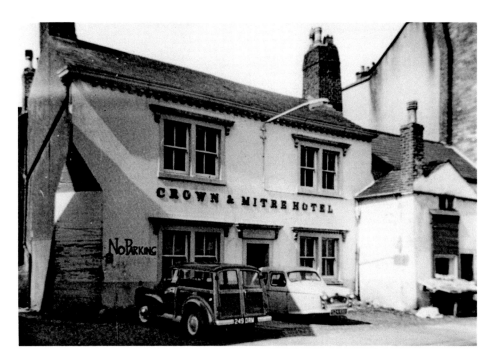

Crown & Mitre

The Crown & Mitre Hotel shortly before demolition. A former coaching Inn, the Crown & Mitre had a large rear yard where a windmill once stood. Pulled down in the 1830s stone from the mill was used to build stables. Next right is Henry Allen's greengrocer's (once the Cross Keys Inn) and the Kildare Hotel.

In the second picture David Bedlington, Wigton's park keeper drives his mower past the entrance to Croft Court. The shops and flats of Lindsay House have replaced the buildings in the earlier picture leaving the Kildare Hotel detached. Built by Edwin Banks in 1886 originally as a Conservative Club the Kildare has sadly closed.

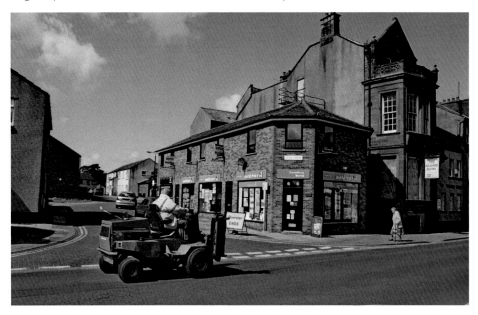

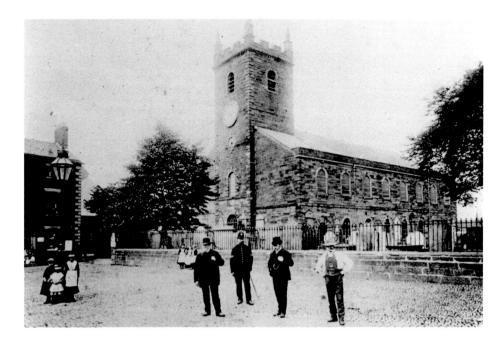

St Mary's

Children pose around the lamp and railings, whilst local worthies stand on the Cornmarket in this fine photograph. Contrast this with the modern picture; the lamp has gone, the Cornmarket is now a car park and the tree beside St Mary's has been felled to reveal scaffolding in front of the Market Hall entrance, and the College of Matrons (Widow's Hospital Cottages) building. Originally founded as a charitable home to house widows of Anglican clergy the Widow's Cottages are now private houses. The churchyard railings have been removed and headstones laid flat in the cemetery garden.

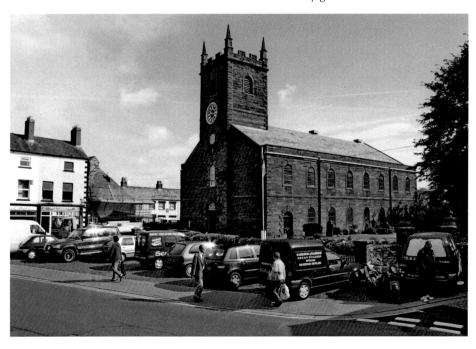

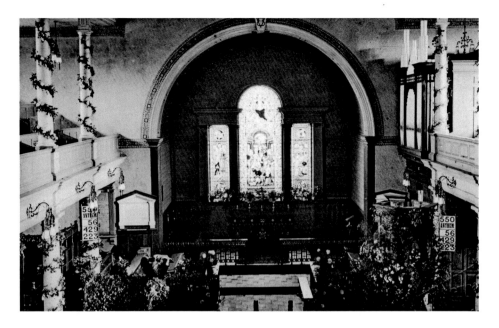

St Mary's Windows

Wigton Parish Church St Mary's decorated for the harvest festival looking towards the east window. Built in 1878 for just under £1500, the church has been under going major restoration under the care of Canon Geoffrey Ravalde. Eight new bells were hung to mark the millennium, the entire roof tiles has been replaced and in 2009 Melvyn Bragg the author and broadcaster gifted 'The Bragg Family Windows', three stained glass windows. Designed by local artist Brian Campbell and manufactured by the Brampton craftsman Alex Graves, the windows combine Wigton's history, commerce and culture with the church's spiritual and pastoral role. This outstanding section shows St Mary's as a beacon in the twilight Wigton landscape.

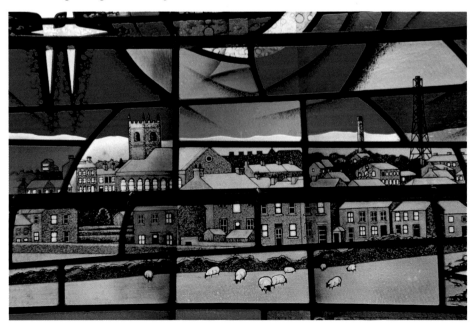

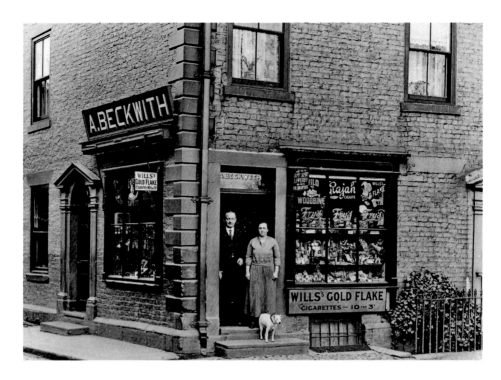

Anthony Beckwith

Anthony Beckwith, his wife and pet dog stand proudly in the doorway of his well-stocked tobacconist and confectionary shop at 49 High Street. The shop was run by Frank Hetherington in the 1930s and in the 1970s Stanley and Ethel Bragg. Today it is a satellite office for the major accountancy firm of Saint & Co, whose Wigton staff (right to left), Chantel Mitchelhill, David Gibson, Daniel Cozens and Liz Gittins stand in the doorway of this much altered property.

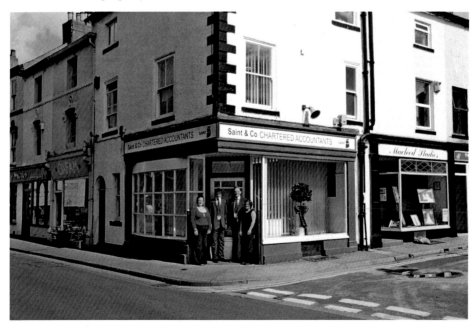

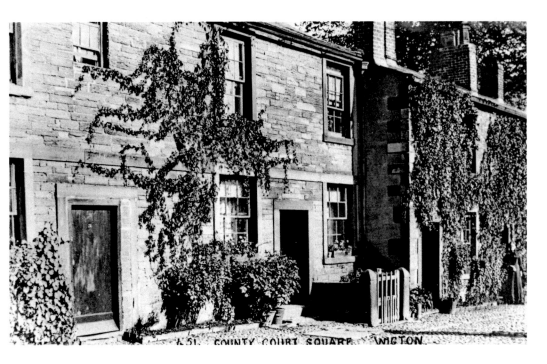

L.51. COUNTY COURT SQUARE. WIGTON.

County Court Square

County Court Square was a pretty cobbled yard of sandstone cottages behind the County Court (now the Community Centre), reached by a short lane from the High Street. Despite a campaign to save the cottages they were pulled down in the 1960s and replaced by a doctor's surgery. The doctors have subsequently moved to Wigton Medical Centre and the surgery is now a dentist's. On the right of the recent picture is the end of the Community Centre Building.

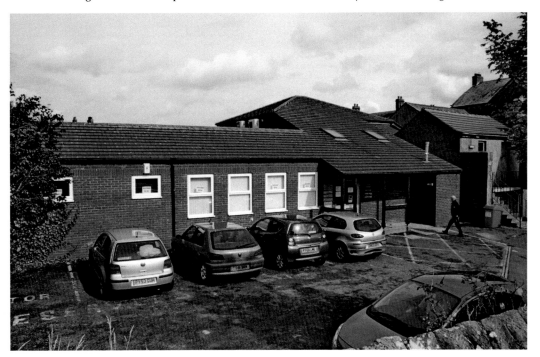

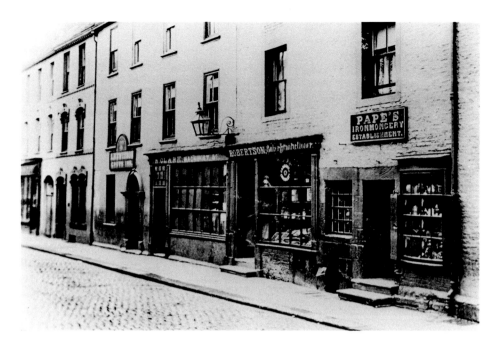

High Street

This section of High Street from the 1880s is an excellent example of Wigton's Georgian architecture. Left is the Crown Inn, landlord Thomas Hewitson, then right the shops of H. Clarke agricultural implement maker and John Robertson baker and confectioner. The last shop is Pape's ironmongery and cycle agent, which continued to trade until the 1950s. Looking at the second photograph apart from the addition of elaborate window decorations little has changed upstairs, but below modernisation has removed the old shop fronts. However recent grants have enabled some restoration, with Bronya of Wigton the exclusive ladies' wear shop, taking the opportunity to install arched window frames matching many of the shop fronts of old.

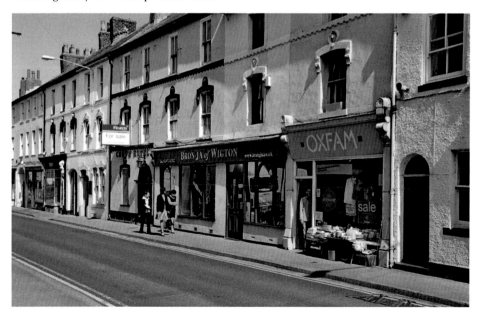

Aird's

Just look at this packed window display as J. Aird & Sons Ltd ironmongers, the do-it-yourself superstore of its day could sell you everything from buckets to the latest gas lighting. In the 1980s the shop was Geoff Wood's jeweller's, later bought by Anne Studholme and Barbara Stoddart and opened as a quality gift shop. To Wigton's surprise the property was painted blue (starting a trend for brightly coloured buildings in the town) and named Toad Hall after the owner's favourite book *The Wind in the Willows*. Elaine Percival is the current owner here pictured in the doorway left with her daughter May, her sister Diane Huddart and her daughter Emma.

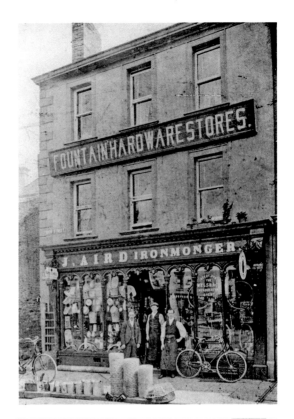

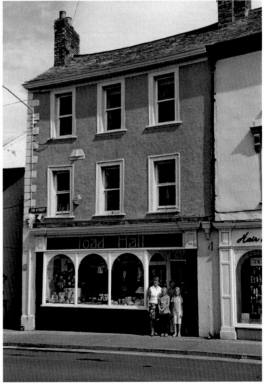

39

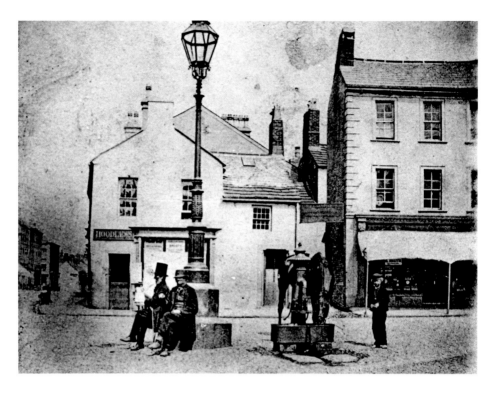

Pump and Lamp

The Market Place is at the heart of Wigton, and at its centre there was once stood an oak cross. Burnt down in 1805 when a bonfire lit to celebrate Lord Nelson's victory at Trafalgar got out of hand, it was replaced by a town pump and gas lamp here photographed in the 1860s. Always a good place to watch the world go by these two gentlemen sit by the lamp outside Henry Hoodless's bookseller and printer's shop, whilst a young boy tends a horse drinking from the pump water trough. Although the pump and lamp have been removed to make way for the Moore Memorial Fountain, as the second photograph shows, even in our busy age, there is still time for two modern gentlemen to enjoy the 'crack' in the Market Place.

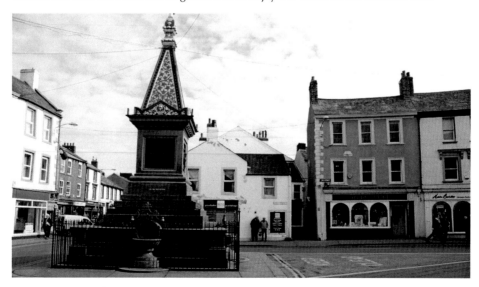

Moore Memorial Fountain

Erected in 1872 by George Moore of Whitehall in memory of his first wife Eliza the Moore Memorial Fountain is Wigton's gem. Here decked out with flags to celebrate Queen Victoria's Diamond Jubilee in 1897, the 33 foot tall fountain built from Shap granite and adorned with four bronze panels depicting acts of mercy (Instructing the Ignorant can be seen here) cost £12,000 to build, a small fortune then. Restored in 2004 with help from The Solway History Society, who paid for new railings, the current picture shows the fountain in all its glory.

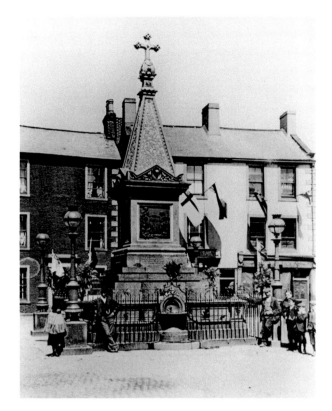

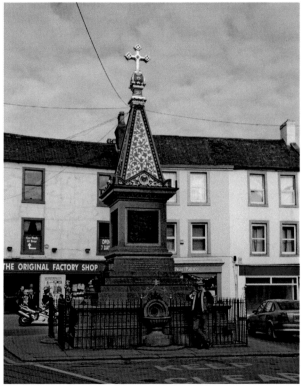

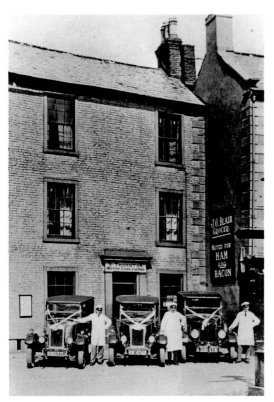

Thornton's Taxis

Dickie Thornton's Taxis decked out for a wedding in the 1930s with drivers (left to right), Rob Cook, George Lawson, and Joe Cook standing outside Dickie's car hire business in Market Place. Shortly after this photograph was taken the ground floor outside wall was removed allowing access to a motor repair garage. When Thornton's closed the premises were converted into Wigton's first large supermarket Walter Wilson's, which has since closed and been replaced by The Original Factory Shop.

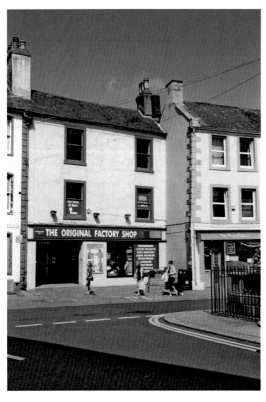

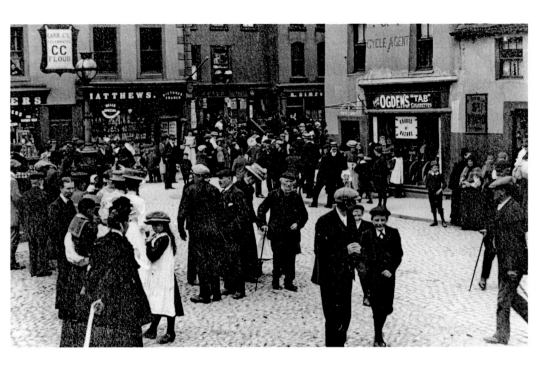

Market Place

Are these people waiting for a carnival or parade? Whatever the reason is, it provides, as usual a good opportunity to catch up on the 'crack'. Now compare this bustling scene of 100 years ago with today's quieter street, the noisy cobbled road replaced with tarmac, the people's attire of caps, suits, long dresses with boots or clogs with today's casual wear. Also the shops; Robert Carruthers with the upstairs advert for Carr's of Silloth flour now an Indian restaurant, and John Matthew's china and glass dealer an estate agent. Joseph Gate stationer is a Greggs baker's shop, and William Payne tobacconist and cycle dealer is also a baker's, Bells of Lazonby.

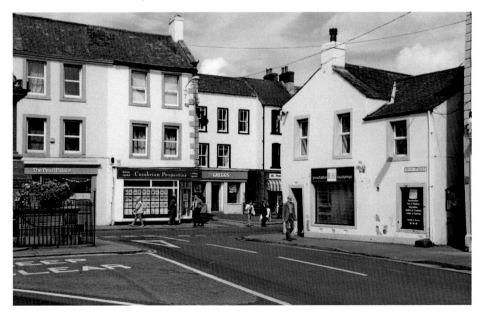

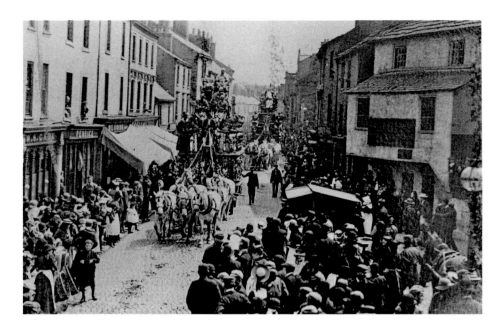

Sanger's Circus

Enormous wagons the height of the High Street rooftops, each pulled by nine white horses announce the arrival of Sanger's Circus into Wigton. A contemporary report from 1893 states that Sanger's travelling circus comprised of 40 wagons towed by 180 horses carrying over 200 performers, equipment and 35 exotic beasts, (including lions, tigers and kangeroos), timed to arrive in Wigton at noon for maximum effect. Yet by that evening the Big Top was up on the Showfields (Barton Laws) and the evening show on. This second picture shows the same view. Note the Dragon Inn on the right, formerly the Kings Head Inn with balcony on the earlier photograph, this is one of Wigton's earliest buildings, once the site of a chapel and hostel dedicated to St Mildred.

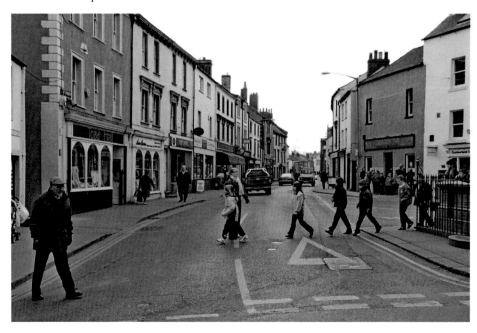

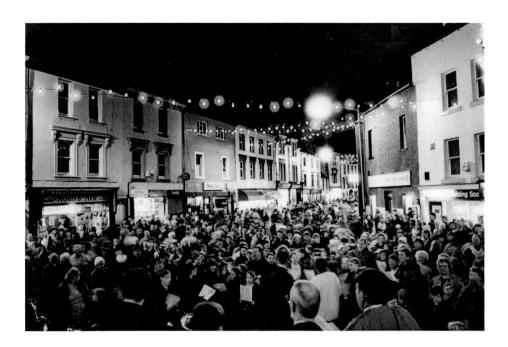

Christmas Celebrations

A Victorian Christmas was special in Wigton, carol singers would go from door to door, the churches would celebrate the birth of the saviour and on Christmas Eve the Wigton Brass Band and Wigton Pipe Band would compete around the Moore Memorial Fountain to see who was best. With the bands long disbanded, Wigton Town Council decided in 1988 to refresh the festivities by holding a carol service and Christmas lights switching on ceremony in Market Place. These two pictures show the crush of people right up High Street in 1988, and the 2009 ceremony with the lit fountain on the left.

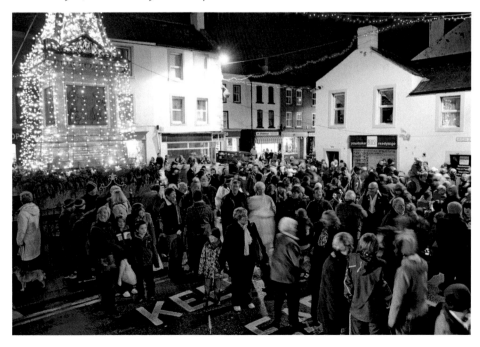

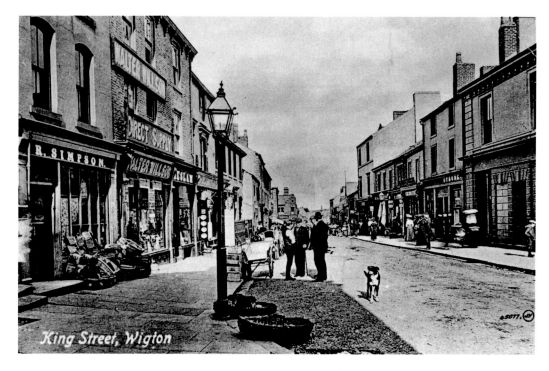

King Street, Wigton

King Street

Baskets of goods from Richard Simpson's merchant's shop, mingle in with hand carts lining King Street, where cars park today. Pedestrians and a dog loiter in the street unconcerned at the traffic, beside the only visible public illumination a solitary gas lamp. In the distance left is the newly built Blue Bell Inn whilst on the right people are window shopping. Today King Street still thrives with many independent shops, but the quantity of motor traffic ensures you stay on the pavement.

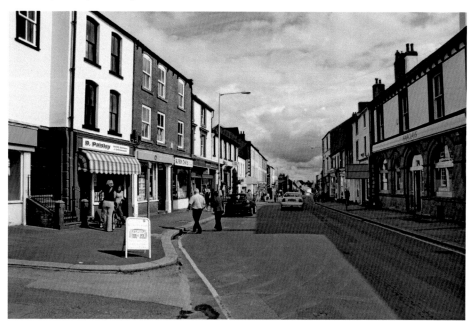

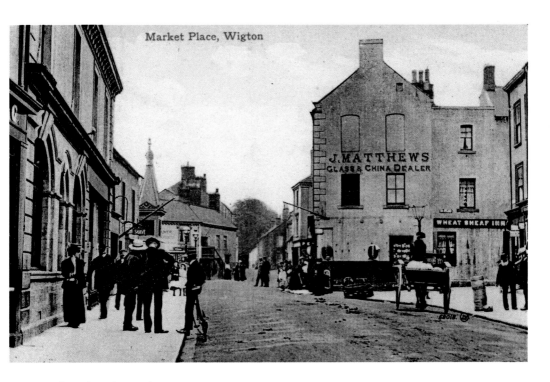

Market Place, Wigton

Market Place from King Street

This 1920s view from King Street looking towards the Market Place shows that cars have yet to dominate Wigton's streets. A boy leans on his bicycle passing the time, whilst a horse and cart trot towards the Wheatsheaf Inn. In the distance is the Moore Memorial Fountain with gas lamps. Left is the former Carlisle & Cumberland Bank now Barclays.

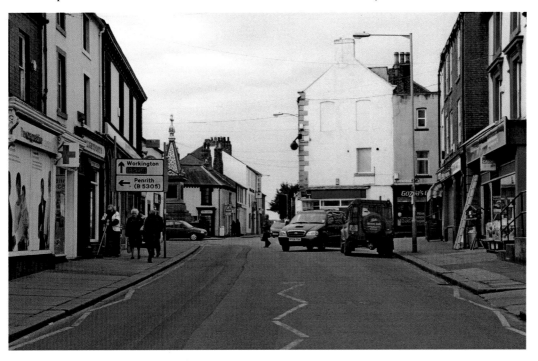

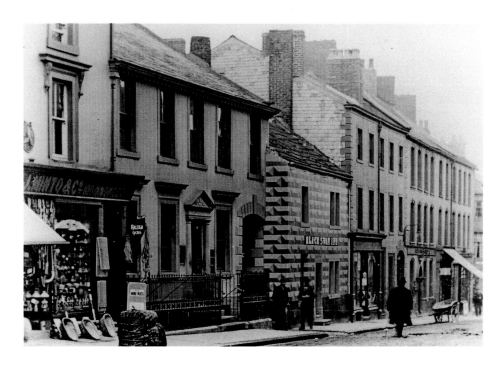

Black Swan

Nearly 120 years have passed since these two pictures were taken. Left on the earlier photograph is William Joseph Minto's ironmonger's, today Saunderson's hardware store, next door is the Cumberland Union Bank now the HSBC. Further right is the Black Swan, cleverly painted to give the illusion of being built from stone blocks. The Black Swan together with part of the former Queens Head Hotel next door is Haldane's grocery store which has recently been acquired from the Co-operative.

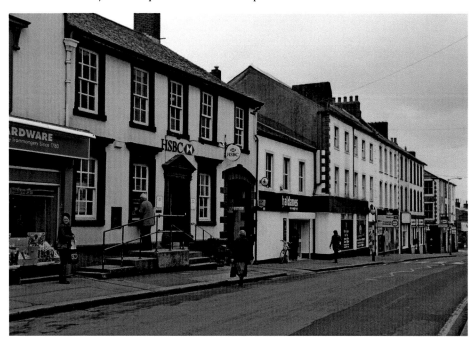

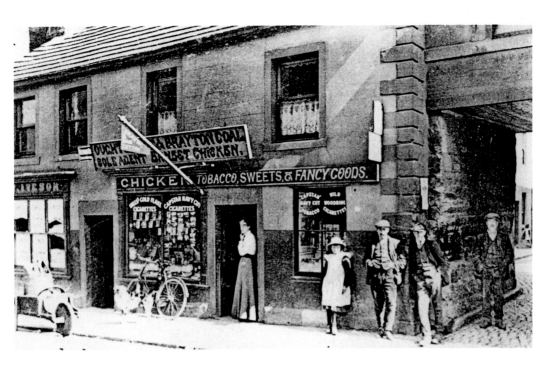

Ernest Chicken

On the corner of King Street and Water Street was Ernest Chicken's tobacconist and coal agent (the coal store was in New Street). Originally an inn named 'The Bold London Apprentice' Chicken's Shop was demolished in 1908 to widen this narrow entrance into Water Street. The second picture shows the outcome with the former central placed doorway now at the property end, and the balcony once attached to the Victoria Hotel gone. Many Wigtonians remember the shop as Ronnie Graham's gentlemen's hairdressers. The Graham family have hung up their scissors, with the barber's now run by Andrew Speak.

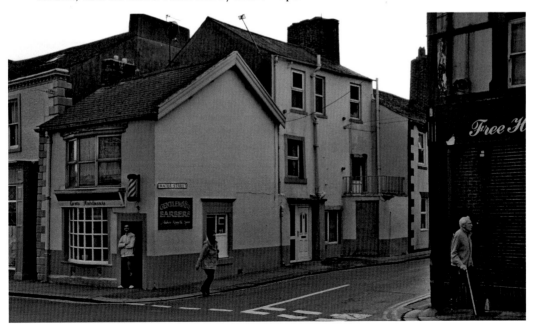

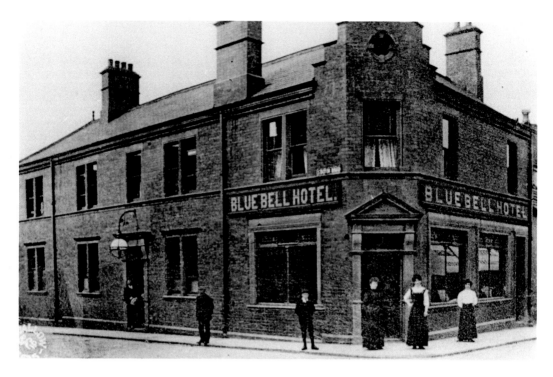

Blue Bell

The first Blue Bell Inn situated at the corner of King Street and Old Lane (Station Road) was pulled down in 1899 to improve access between the streets. The new Blue Bell Hotel pictured here was built of red brick by the Maryport Brewery Company as a replacement for the inn. Ironically this Blue Bell Hotel also became a highway hazard jutting out into King Street and was demolished during further road widening in 1959. A bus station and office then occupied the site for many years before closing. The office later became an Allerdale Council Office before being relocated to the 'Local Links' complex. Now the building is a cleaning business, V. S. Cleaning Service with the former Blue Bell yard a car park.

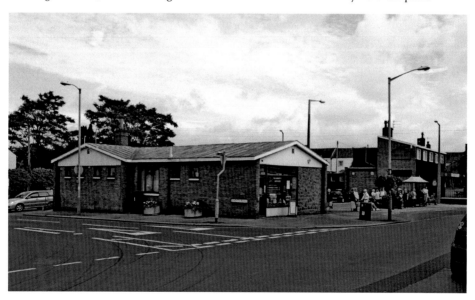

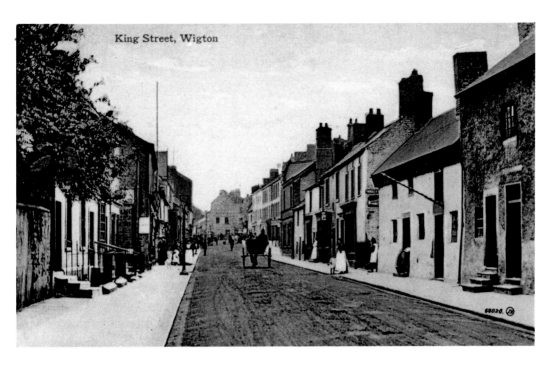

King Street, Wigton

Thackey House

A horse and cart amble up the wrong side of King Street in this 1915 picture. Right are former weavers' cottages with the railed steps leading down to damp cellars where the loom was worked. Left with the barber's pole is Thackey House, a former 'Jerry Shop' licensed to sell ale but not spirits, the property once had a thatched roof, replaced by iron sheeting in this picture. On the second picture all the properties on the right up to Station Road have gone, replaced by the Throstle's Nest pub, a car park and V. S. Cleaning Service shop.

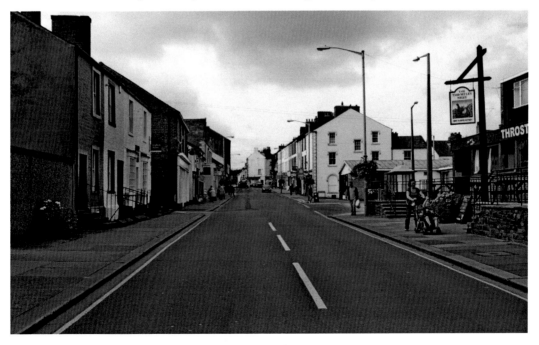

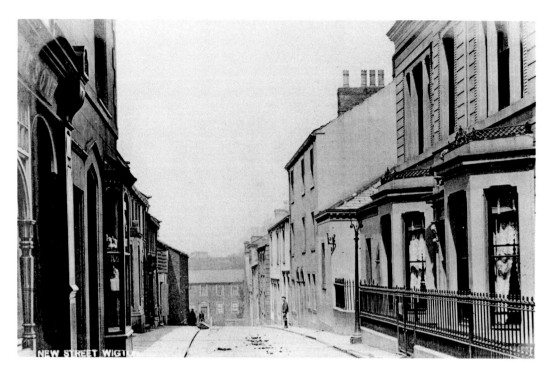

New Street

A side street leading from King Street to Station Road, New Street was only 'new' in the 1760s when building plots were sold off by the Lord of the Manor. A peaceful street many of the properties are little changed. These views also show the Station Road Police Station and Magistrates' Court at the bottom of the hill built in 1908.

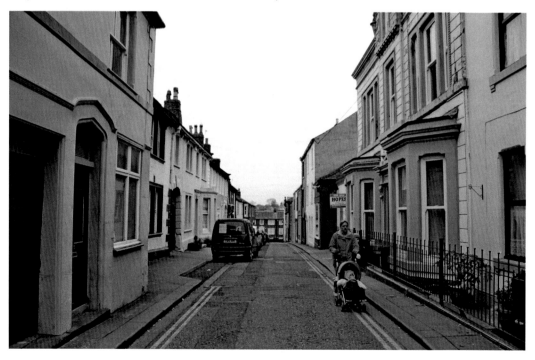

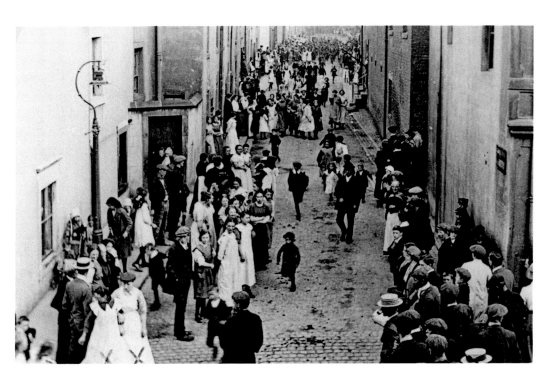

Water Street

Water Street viewed from the balcony that once connected the Victoria Hotel with Ernest Chicken's shop. In the distance between the tightly-packed houses the residents await the arrival in the distance of soldiers from the Lonsdale Battalion on a 1915 recruitment march. No doubt many signed up eager for excitement, and to get away from the poverty of Water Street. The second view shows few changes to the entrance of Water Street, but further down the street the back-to-back cottages have been demolished, with the car park entrance visible past the Victoria Hall on the right (right background on the newer picture). On the horizion is Highmoor Tower which would once have looked down on the poorest part of Wigton.

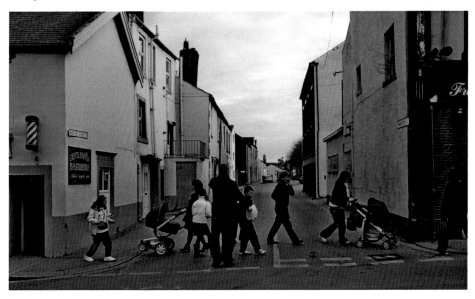

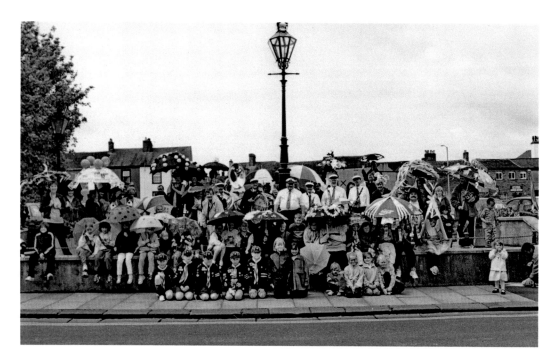

Umbrella Parade

Starting with breakfast in the Market Hall, then parading through Wigton in a New Orleans style customised umbrella parade to the jazz beat of the 'The Lairds of Dixieland' was a regular Easter event for Wigton children in the early noughties, and yet another excuse for the fancy dress parades Wigtonians adore. This 2001 picture has the participants posed beside the pump (hidden) and lamp in Water Street. The second picture shows the pump and lamp after their many travels, settled in front of the Water Street car park. In the distance is the back of High Street properties.

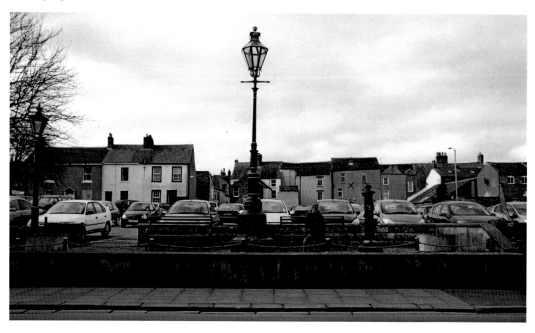

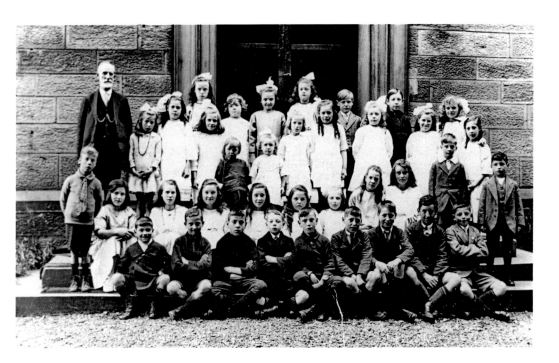

United Reformed Church

The 28th June 2009 was a sad day as Wigton's United Reformed Church closed its doors after 175 years. A dwindling congregation together with the need for expensive renovation to the church, left the diocese no option than to close. In 1923 these children resplendent in their Sunday best clothes posed in the church doorway, would have thought this unbelievable. To these children and thousands more the church was a spiritual home on Sundays and an educational necessity as lessons were taught in the cellar schoolroom through the week. Recently the church has been purchased with the intention of converting it into a computer museum.

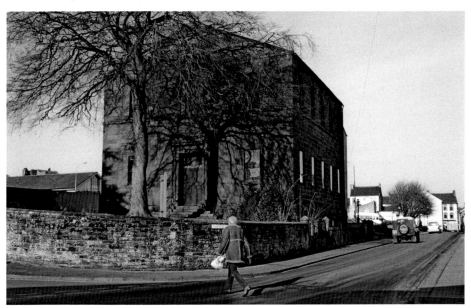

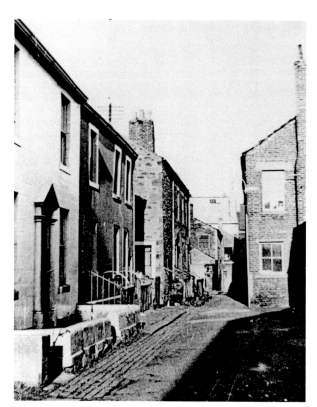

Church Street

This is one of the few old photographs of Church Street that survive. Winding from King Street to St Mary's Church and parallel with Water Street, Church Street was once a hive of industry. Packed with tanneries, warehouses and back-to-back houses (some with a family on each floor and a hand loom in the cellar), many of the residents lived in poverty. By the 1960s most of the area had been pulled down and replaced by Water Street car park which can partly be seen in the background of the newer picture. Few houses were spared excepting the terrace on the left of these pictures.

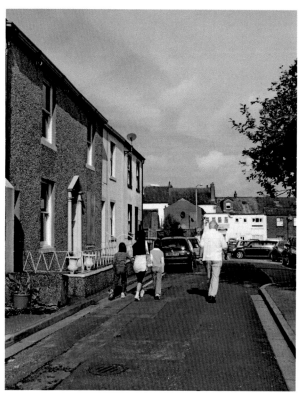

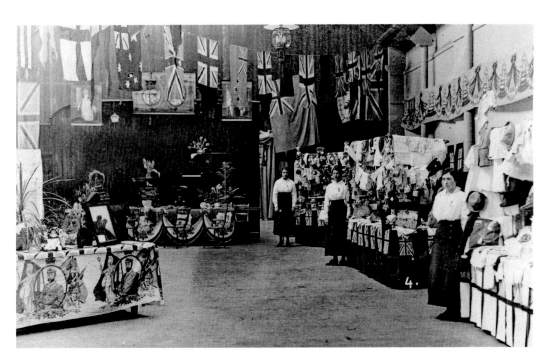

Market Hall

Built in 1882 to provide a covered market for the sale of agricultural produce the Market Hall on Church Street soon became a social centre in Wigton. Here decorated in 1916 with flags and images of King George V is the Market Hall prepared for a patriotic Empire Bazaar. Selling needlework and fancy goods the bazaar raised £170 for the soldiers fighting in the First World War. Recently the Market Hall has been refurbished at a cost of £735,000. The second picture shows the modernised entrance (after the scaffolding has been removed – see St Mary's picture), with the College of Matrons on the right.

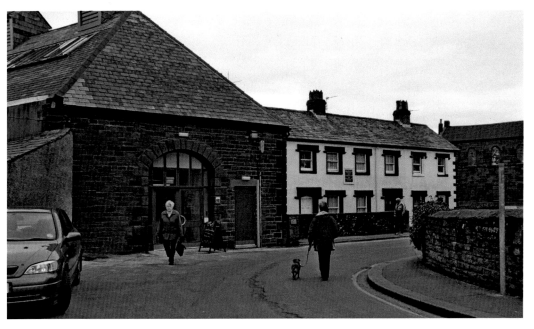

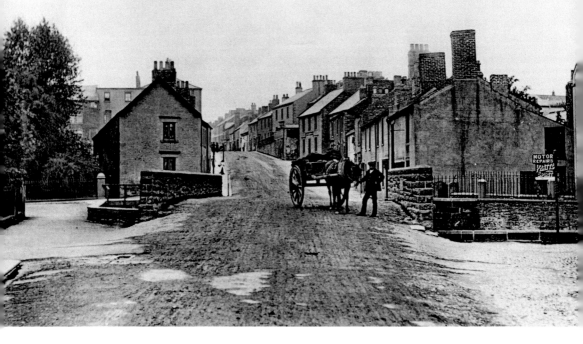

Burnfoot

Looking towards King Street a carter poses for the photographer on Burnfoot Bridge. Left in the distance are the three-storey houses of Market Hill and opposite right across the road the Black a Moor Hotel. On the extreme right is the Duck Inn (now a private house) beside a sign pointing to Edward Mason's garage, now replaced by the colourful ATS sign.

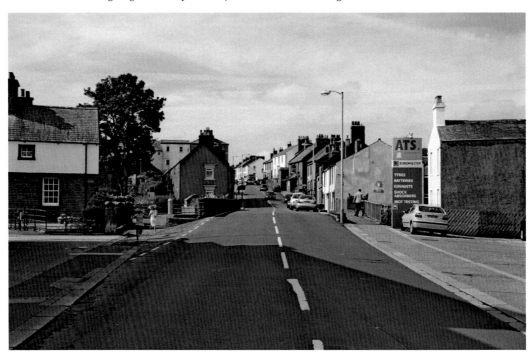

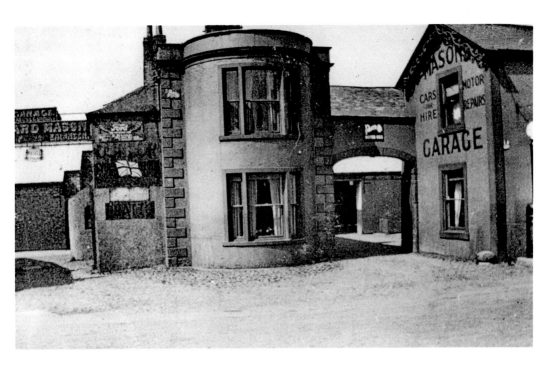

Edward Mason's

Edward Mason's garage beside Speet Gill was once the site of Burnfoot Brewery, which had owned eighteen pubs including the Blue Bell Hotel and Greyhound in Wigton. Many of the brewery buildings survive in this 1930s picture, which had consisted of two cottages, a brewing house and bottling plant. Over the years Mason's incorporated the brewery buildings into the garage as it was enlarged, until bought out by Associated Tyre Services who have stamped their corporate image on the garage.

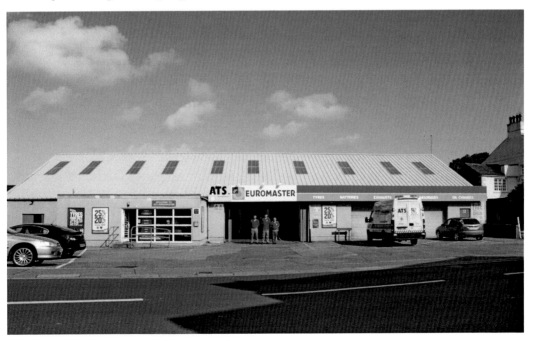

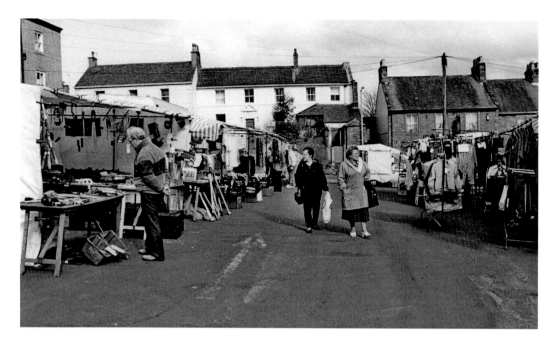

Market Hill

2001 was a year of devastation in Cumbria. Foot and Mouth, one of the most virulent diseases known to mankind, was destroying Cumbria's livestock. To check the pestilence, movement of farm animals was forbidden and Hope's mart closed. No access was allowed on the mart premises so the Friday traders' market was moved to the site of Wigton's former nineteenth-century market place, Market Hill, pictured here. With the reopening of Hope's the Friday market returned to the mart, and Market Hill reverted to a car park. In the background of these two pictures is the former free grammar school built in 1730 (centre) with the Black a Moor Hotel right.

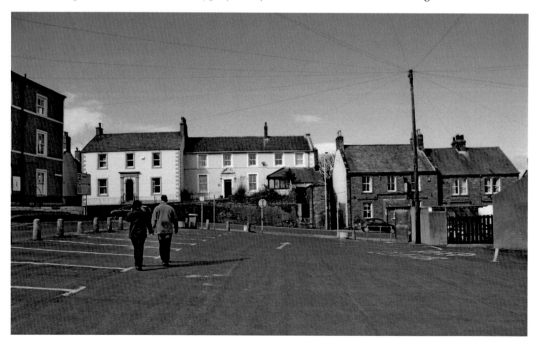

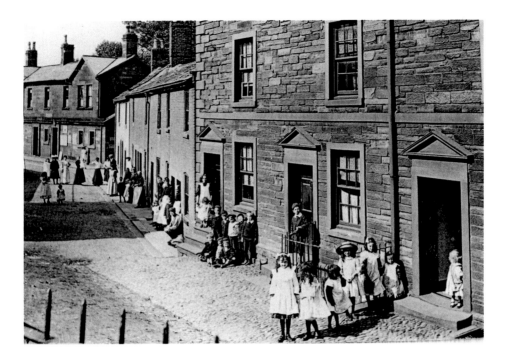

Market Hill Cottages

Once known as 'Toon End' Market Hill in the 1850s was a place to be avoided, inhabited by labourers, weavers and paupers. By the 1900s the neighbourhood had improved as this charming Edwardian picture of well-dressed children standing on their doorsteps shows. Compare this with the current occupants also standing beside or near their homes. The middle cottages have gone replaced by the flats of Hodgsons Close, whilst the two storey former police station on the left is now private housing.

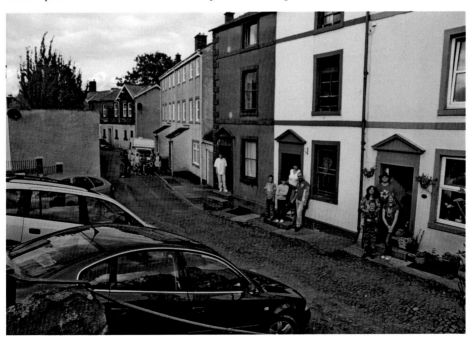

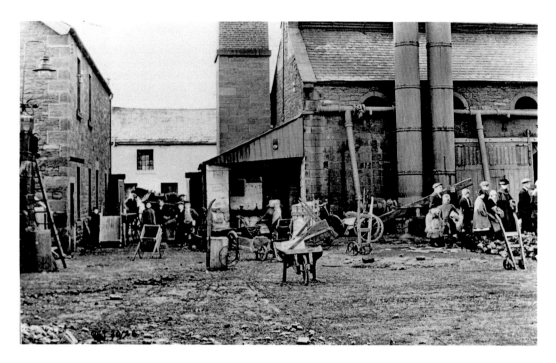

Tenters

Wigton Gas Works was built in Tenters for £4000 in 1831. At first Victorian Wigton was reluctant to experiment with the new fuel, preferring to cook over the fire and use candle light. But gas eventually caught on and the gas works enlarged in 1856. This picture taken during the 1926 General Strike shows householders queueing for coke as coal was unavailable. On the left of the older picture is the manager's house, the only structure still remaining (still known today as the Gas House and on the left of the second picture). Whilst the cottage behind the horse is the end cottage on the right of the recent photograph.

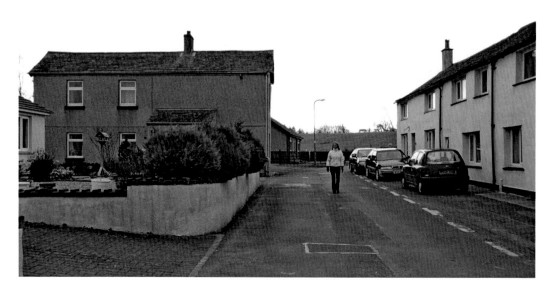

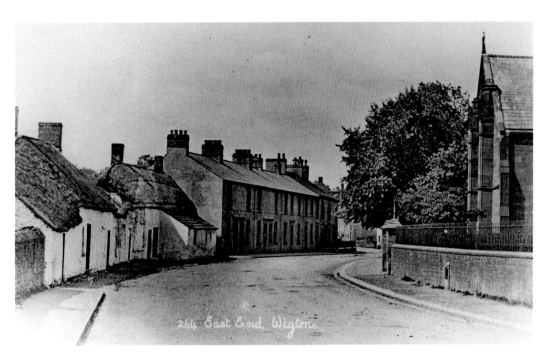

East End

East End looking towards Burnfoot. On the left is the clay dabbin White Row cottages. Built around a timber frame, the walls were made of clay dug from Kirkland Clay Dubs, mixed with straw and coated with cow manure and horsehair (for waterproofing) and then whitewashed. Finally a thatch roof was added. These houses would have been very poor dwellings, in sharp contrast to the magnificence of St Cuthbert's Church opposite. White Row has been pulled down and new properties occupy the site.

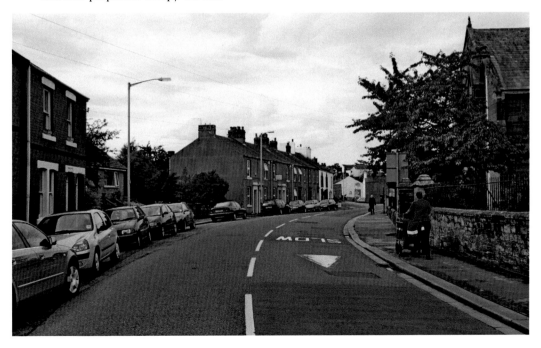

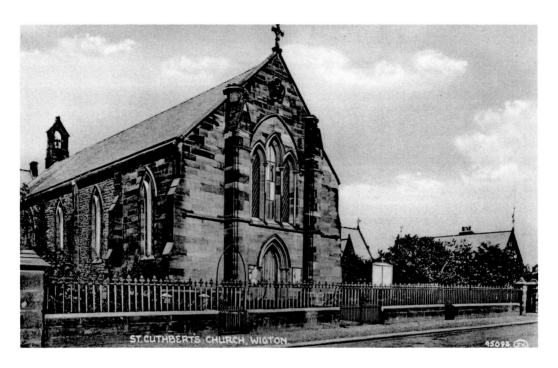

St Cuthbert's

A comparison of these two views of St Cuthbert's Church shows few changes over the years. Built from a design by the architect Bonomi in 1837, a convent (whose roof is just visible behind the notice board) was added in 1856. Mainly funded by Elizabeth Aglionby of Wigton Hall and opened by nuns from the Sisters of Mercy order who had cared for wounded soldiers during the Crimean War, the convent closed in 2002. However the school they founded remains and St Cuthbert's Church continues to thrive.

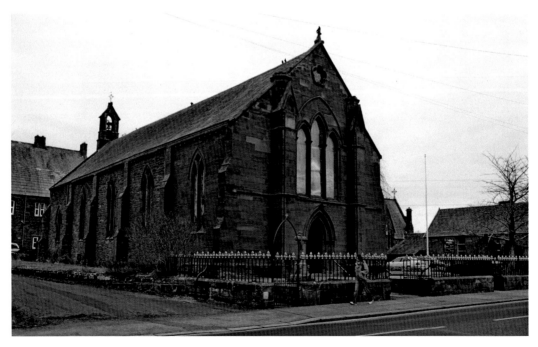

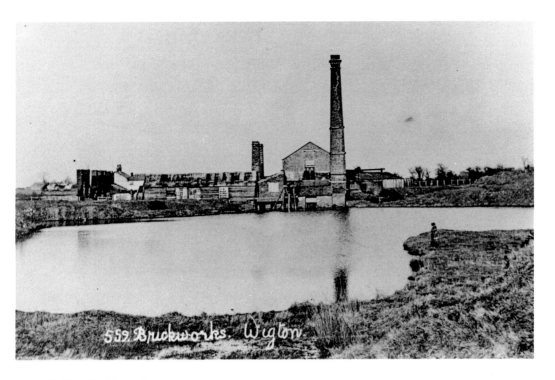

Kirkland Brickworks

Directly east of St Cuthbert's Church lies the Clay Dubs. Once the source of clay to built dabbin houses, by the 1830s the Briggs family had constructed a brickworks manufactory on site. Closed in the early twentieth century, the hollow left after clay extraction was used as a fishpond, swimming pool and, in winter, a skating rink. Eventually it became a refuse tip which has now been cleaned and landscaped. The modern view is of the former site from Kirkland Road.

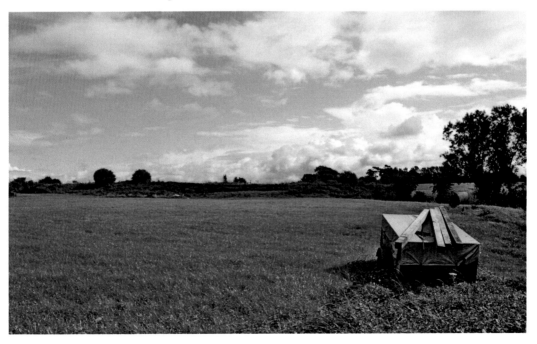

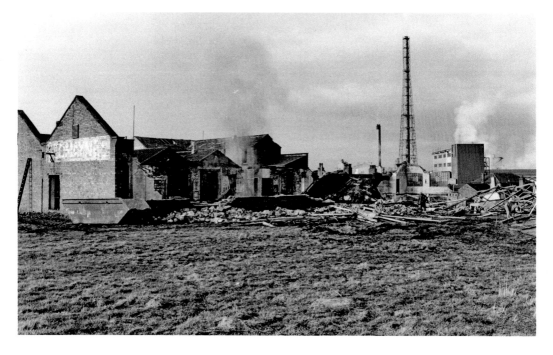

Redmayne's

Samuel Redmayne founded his made to measure gentlemen's tailors in 1868, opening a new factory on Station Road in 1875. By the 1950s Redmayne & Sons had twenty-four branch shops and three factories, whilst been granted a Royal Warrant in 1968. By 1981 the business had declined and the Station Road factory closed. In 1987 the factory now derelict was being demolished when this photograph was taken. Today the site is occupied by new houses and Somerfield supermarket. In the background is Innovia Films.

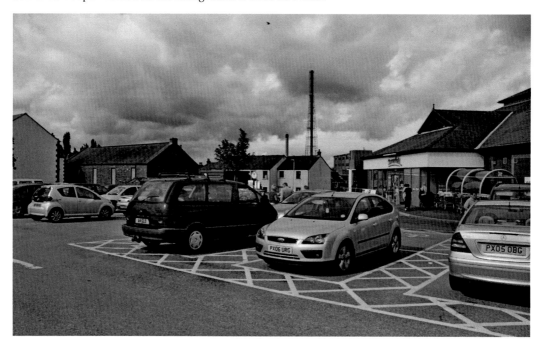

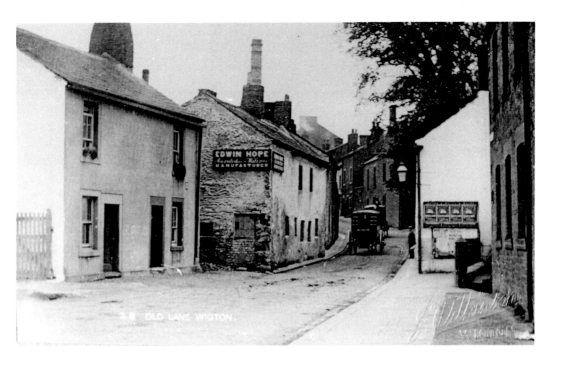

Old Lane

An early view of Old Lane (now Station Road) looking towards King Street. Better known as 'Bog Road' due to an open sewer which flowed to the River Wiza, it is perhaps not the most hygenic location for Edwin Hope's soft drinks manufactory which had once been the Parish poorhouse (an early institution to house the poor before workhouses). On the right was John Dalton's tannery whose business would have added to the noxious waste entering the open drain. In 1882 proper sewers were installed and over the years many of these properties demolished. Today Len Green's electrical workshop on the left of the second picture occupies the site of Edwin Hope's.

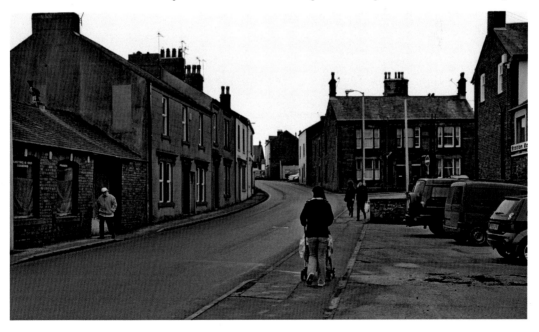

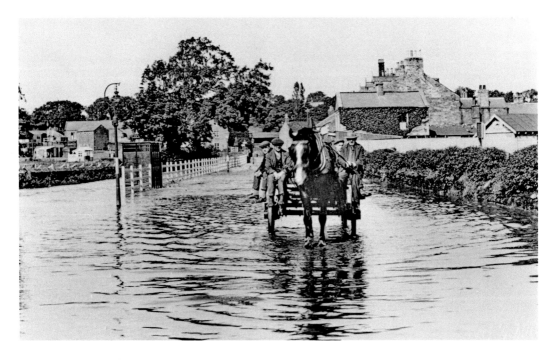

Station Road Flood

In the early hours of 20 September 1926, sheet lightening lit up the night sky and torrential rain fell on Wigton. By daybreak the storm had ended, leaving Wigton's rivers overflowing. Speet Gill burst its banks at Tenters and Burnfoot flooding houses, whilst the River Wiza flooded Station Road. This photograph taken that afternoon shows Tommy Miller with his horse and cart transporting passengers through the Station Road flood into town. Today despite modern flood defences Station Road still occasionally floods, a situation that seemed very unlikely when this summer picture looking toward the railway bridge was taken.

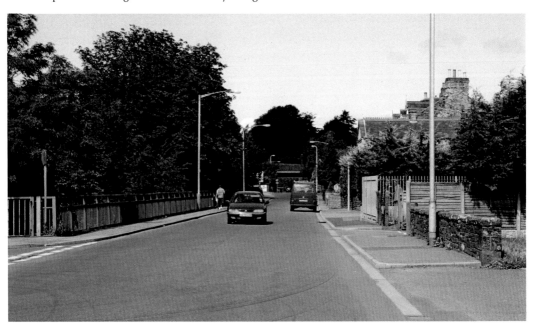

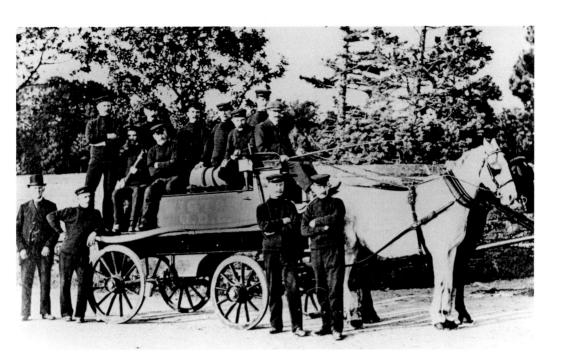

Fire Brigade

Wigton's first fire engine was a simple cart with mounted hand pump, stored in St Mary's porch. Upon discovery of a fire the Church bells were rung and it was 'all hands to the pump'. In 1857 Wigton people raised money to purchase a horse-drawn Merryweather steam fire engine, equipped with boiler, lead-lined water reservoir and manned by volunteers as pictured. Today Wigton has a modern fire station, with two appliance bays and highly trained firefighters on Station Road. Sited directly opposite their main concern the Innovia factory, which uses toxic solvents and corrosives in its manufacturing process. Some of the brigade are pictured here beside a Volvo engine, re-enacting their forebears' pose.

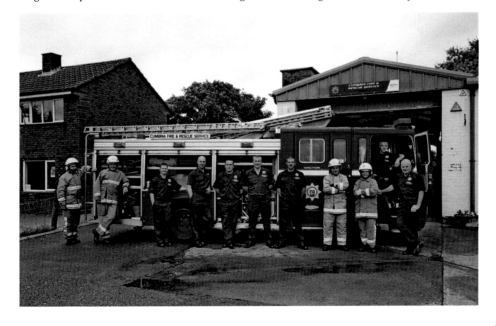

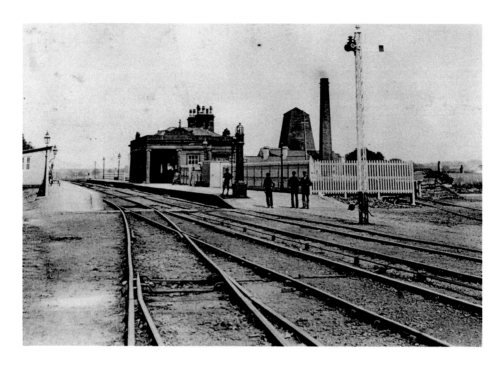

Railway Station

Wigton Railway Station was built in 1845, two years after the line connecting Maryport to Carlisle was complete. Left of the station is a gas-lit shelter for passengers to Carlisle, then the fine sandstone ticket office, with water pump and behind a disused windmill (note no sails) and tannery chimney. The ticket office was dismantled in the early nineteenth century to make way for a modern building, and sold to the Senhouse family at Netherhall Maryport, as a summerhouse. As you can see the current replacement building is a poor substitute. Recently a Friends of Wigton Station group has formed to improve the station facilities.

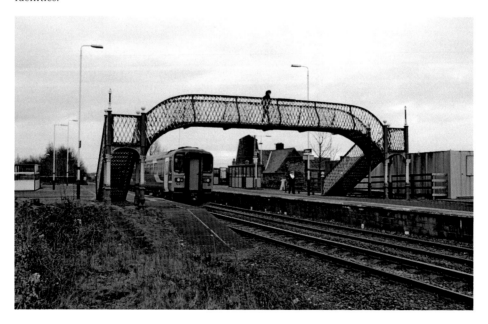

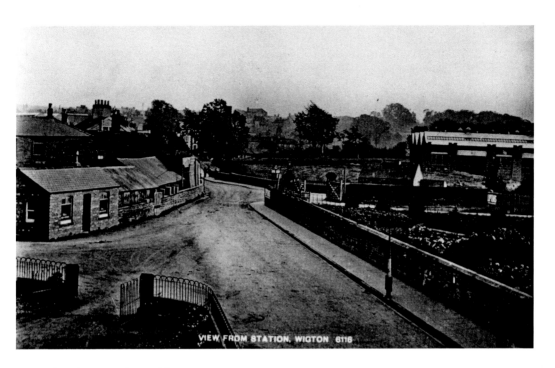

VIEW FROM STATION, WIGTON 6118

View from Station Bridge

A 1920s summer view from the railway bridge down Station Road. Right is the Preserve Manufactures Ltd works. At its peak the jam factory manufactured 100 tons of preserve daily, exported by rail throughout the country. On the left is J. Hartley timber merchants. The second winter view clearly shows St Mary's tower on the horizon. The jam factory had closed in 1927 and its remaining buildings are integrated into Innovia Films, whilst J. Hartley's sawmill is now a Cumbria County Council office.

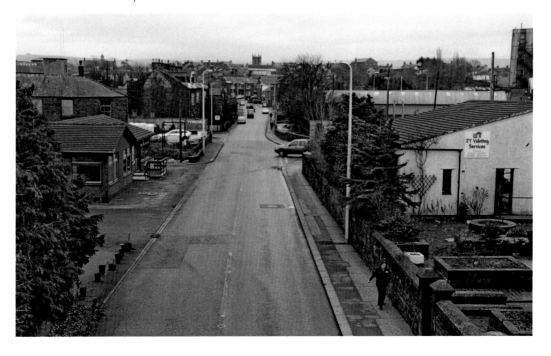

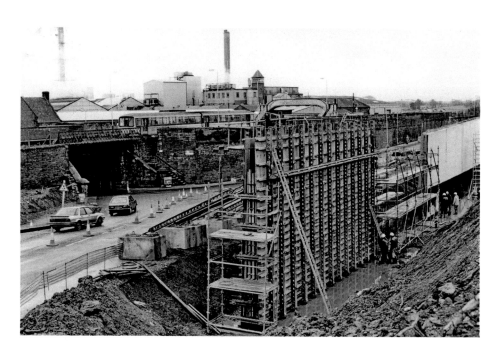

Wigton Bypass

Wigton has sufferered from that modern affliction, traffic congestion since 1938 when the first town bypass was proposed. But it was not until 1992 that work began on diverting the A595 Carlisle to West Cumbria road away from the town centre. This picture shows the ongoing work. Right is the railway bridge above Station Road with the train to Carlisle. On the horizon is the station footbridge and factory. Whilst in the foreground is the massive steel structure built to hold back the steep slope of Station Hill. The second picture is taken from the top of this structure which has been dressed in sandstone.

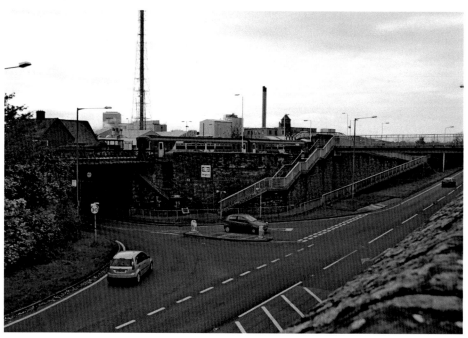

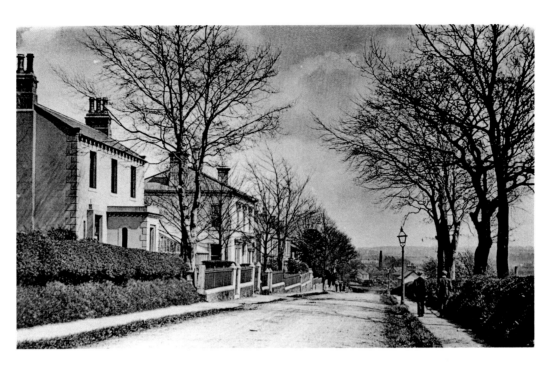

Station Hill
Two men stroll down the hill towards Station Road. Left is Ashley House (now obscured by trees) and then Brasfort House. Mainly built in the 1840s the superior houses of Station Hill were erected as a residential suburb overlooking the town. The recent bypass has effectively separated Station Hill from Wigton, but the location remains desirable enjoying extensive views over the town.

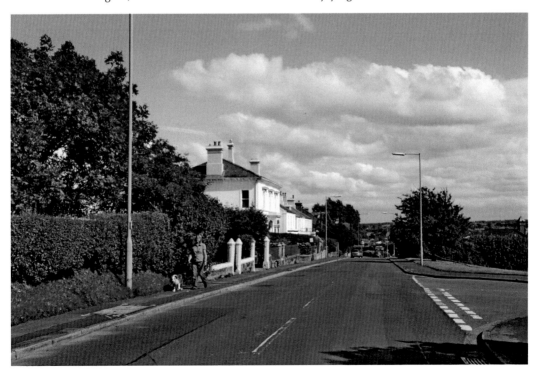

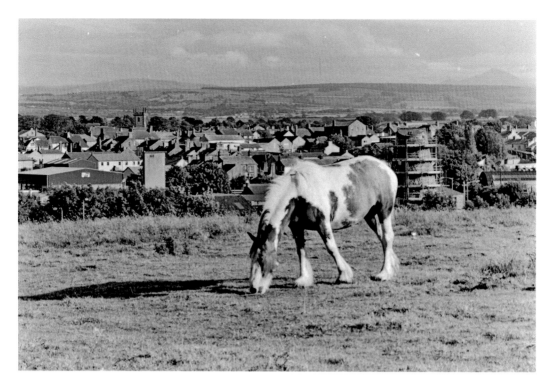

Cross Lane

This 1997 view from Cross Lane depicts Wigton nestled on the Solway Plain, below the Caldbeck Fells (left) and Skiddaw (right). St Mary's tower is clearly visible, whilst scaffolding is attached to Sloan's Mill once the tallest windmill in Cumberland, and now Station Joinery a carpenter's workshop. Since then this picturesque view has been lost, blocked by the new residential estate of Standing Stone Heights built in 2004 to fulfill Wigton's need for more housing.

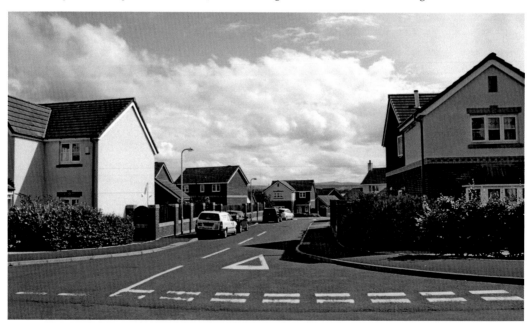

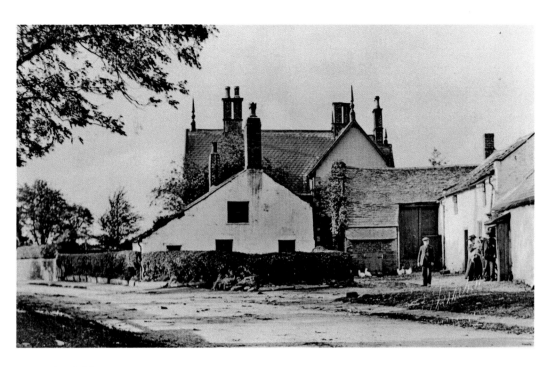

The Gables

Standing beside the road to Oulton, The Gables (the large property behind the cottage) built in 1851 would have been one of the few residential properties at Standingstone, surrounded by much of Wigton's industry. The nearby Wiza provided water for a dye house, brewery and Isaac Pattinson & Sons textile works, whilst Black Beck fed Halliley McAlpine & Co print works, all close by. By 1925 most of the industry was long gone and the industrial ponds left on Cross Lane and Standingstone filled in. Today the Gables has little changed, but the left side cottage has gone, whilst hens are no longer kept in the yard.

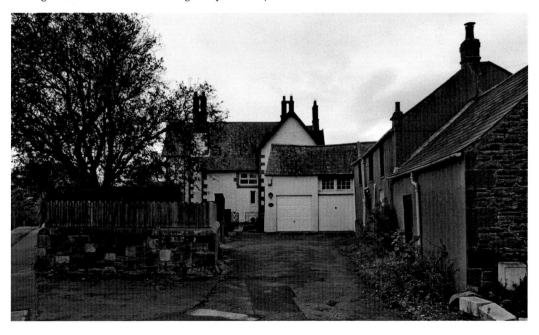

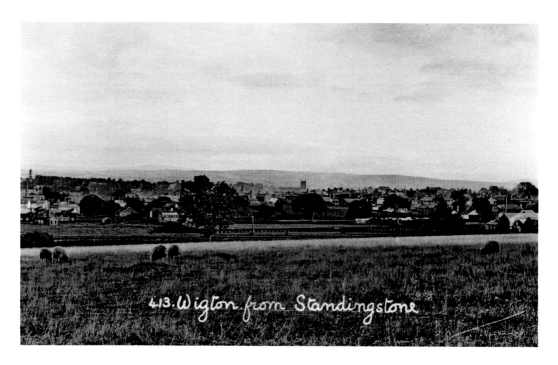

413. Wigton from Standingstone

Wigton from Standingstone

Wigton in the 1900s from Standingstone. On the far left is Highmoor Tower, then right behind the second pair of sheep the chimney of Carr & White Preserve Manufacturers Ltd who prospered during the First World war supplying Wigton jam to the troops. Dominating the centre is St Mary's tower and on the far right a tannery chimney. In the foreground is the Maryport & Carlisle Railway Co track. In the second picture autumn trees now obscure the railway track and much of the town, yet Highmoor and St Mary's tower are still visible.

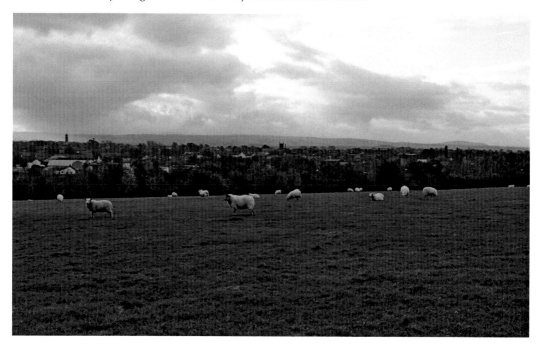

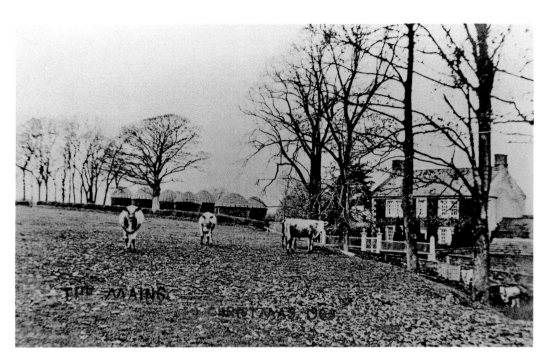

The Mains

This lovely rural view of the The Mains situated between Standingstone and Spittal was posted as a Christmas card in 1908. Note the abundant haystacks, the well-fed stock and traditional Cumberland farmhouse hardly changed today. Today The Mains is a modern farm owned by the Wharton family which specialise in pork production. The pigsties are further down the lane (off the picture right).

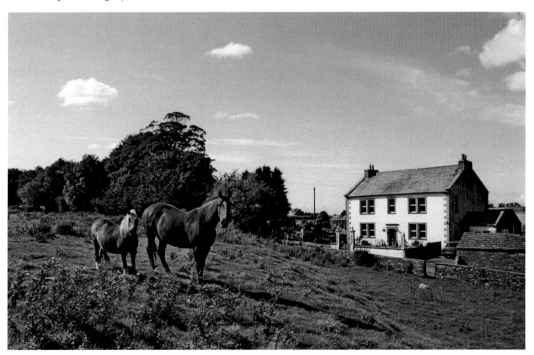

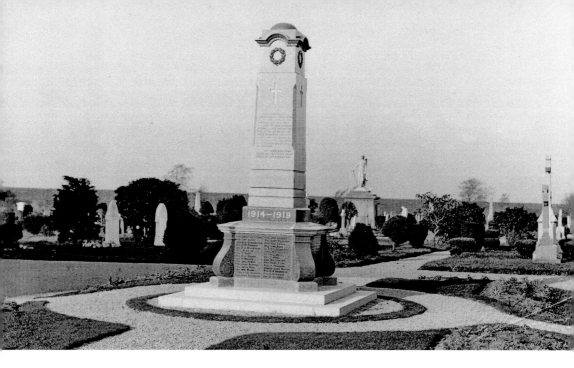

Cemetery

In 1878 Jane Matthews of Wigton Hall donated five acres of Aikhead pasture for a cemetery. In 1920 the centotaph illustrated in these two pictures was unveiled in remembrance of the 119 men and one women who died in the First World War. Right of the older picture (left on the current photograph) is the Bank's Mausoleum with the statue of Justice standing on top. As always Wigton cemetery remains a peaceful place with pristine gardens.

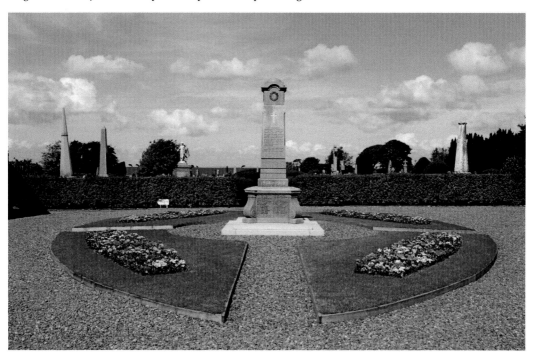

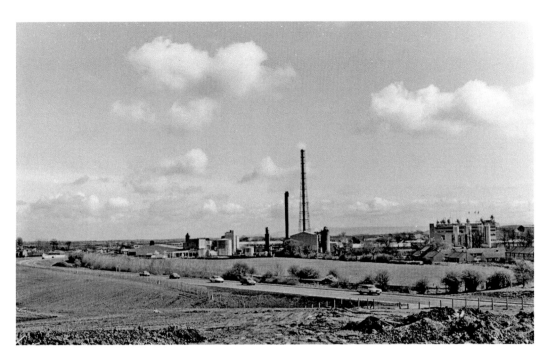

The Factory

From Longhead snapped within weeks of the 1993 bypass opening. The site, once part of the jam works was bought by British New-Wrap Company in 1933 to manufacture cellulose film, since then it has been taken over several times and is now owned by Innovia Films, but known to the people of Wigton as simply 'The Factory'. In this picture is the 325-foot chimney built in 1966 to take noxious chemical fumes away from the town, whilst right is the 1970s new factory built to manufacture polypropylene film. The winter scene shows how tree planting has almost hidden The Factory with only part of works, and a lorry visible through the hedge.

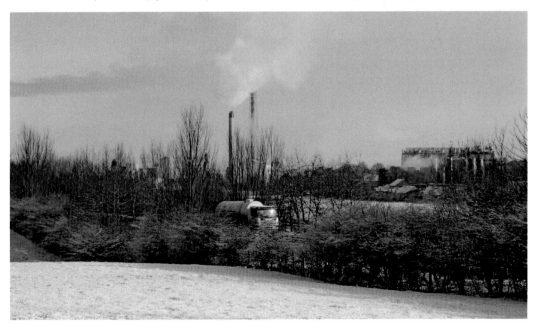

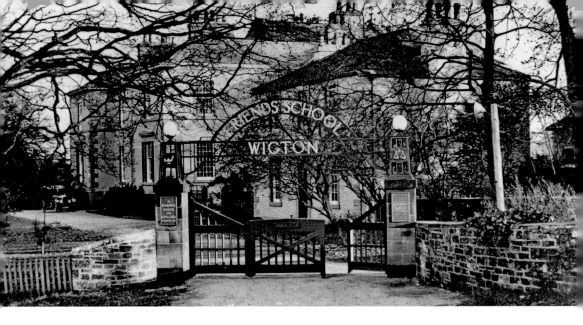

Brookfield, West Gate

In 1815 the Society of Friends (Quakers) leased Highmoor Cottage and opened it as school for seventeen scholars. By 1827 increasing student numbers meant Highmoor Cottage was too small, so a purpose built school capable of educating eighty pupils was built for £3602 2s 3d at Brook-in-Field and named Brookfields. This fine view shows Brookfield School behind the West Gate erected in 1932 in memoriam of Joseph J. Jopling headmaster (1893-1923). The second picture shows that the gate, sign and lamps have gone, whilst the remaining visible part of the school is now a private residence.

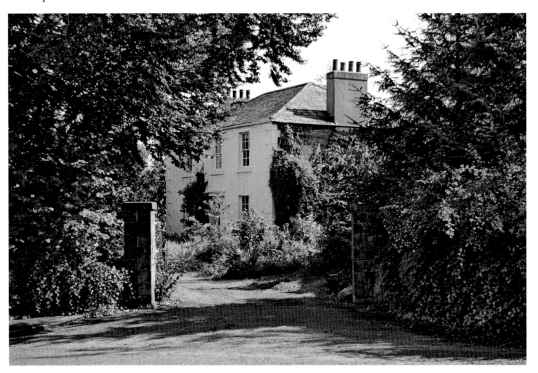

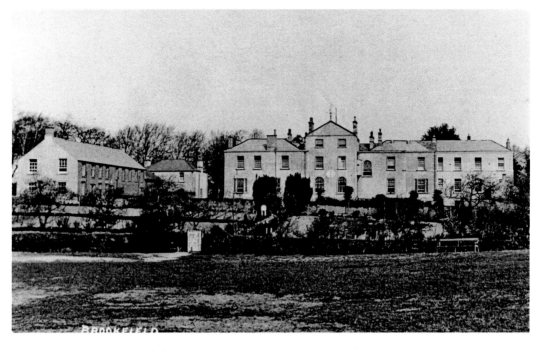

Brookfield School

In 1985 Brookfield School's pupils totalled less than 100. As the school needed 120 pupils to financially continue, the governors had no choice than to sell to Lime House private school at Dalston. Brookfield continued as a private school until 1989 when a fire swept through the buildings. Most of the school was subsequently demolished, with the few remaining buildings incorporated into the new Brookfields housing estate. This old picture from the back of the school shows the imposing three-storey lecture hall in the centre, then left the library and classrooms. Today only the classrooms can be seen in the second picture, situated at the end of this new cul-de-sac.

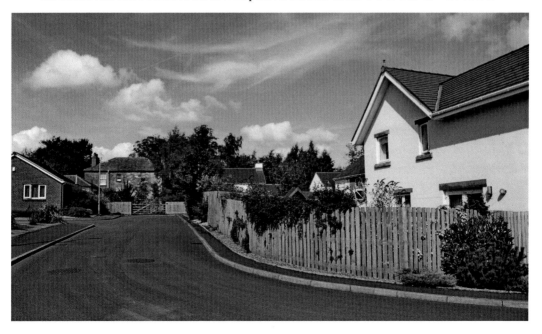

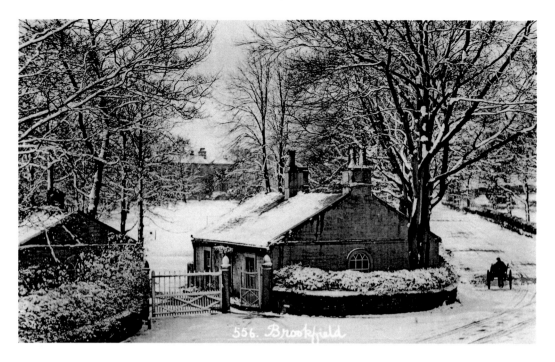

Brookfield Lodge

A spectacular winter view from West Road of the northern entrance to Brookfield and its lodge. At the end of the tree-lined avenue can just be made out Brookfield School in the snow, whilst right a horse and cart trot down the road towards Wigton. Many of the trees survive today, but the lodge has been pulled down and the entrance now leads to Brookfields housing estate.

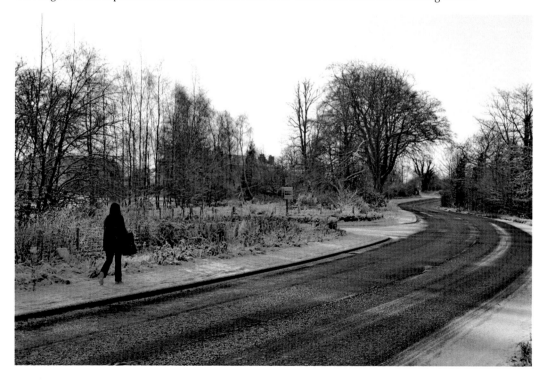

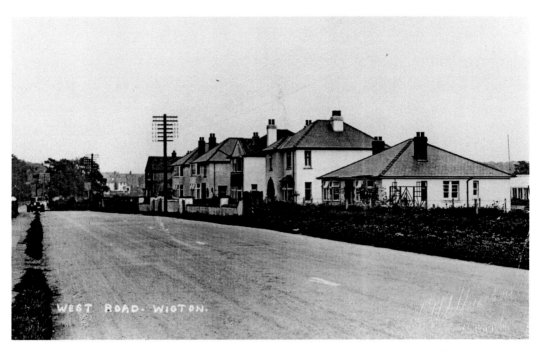

West Road

By the 1930s the reluctance of the previous decade for people to move to the outskirts of Wigton had disappeared, as new desirable family homes with gardens were being built. These houses on West Road between Skiddaw View and Brookfield are typical. The second picture shows the properties today little changed.

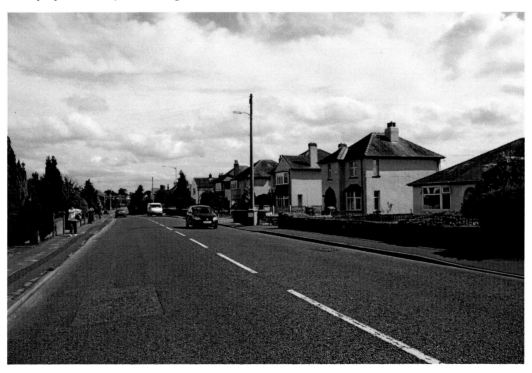

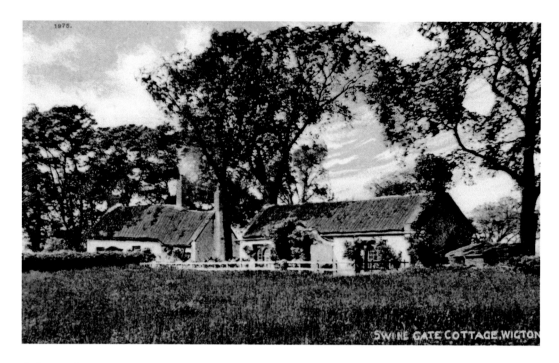

Swingate Cottages

Once isolated at the western edge of Wigton, the two former yeoman farmers houses of Swingate, were beside a forest where swine could feed on acorns. Today Swingate Cottages have been tastefully modernised since this 1907 picture, and although some features have gone, the original stone window surrounds survive on The Nook cottage (right) as seen on the second picture here photographed from the garden of Bow Cottage.

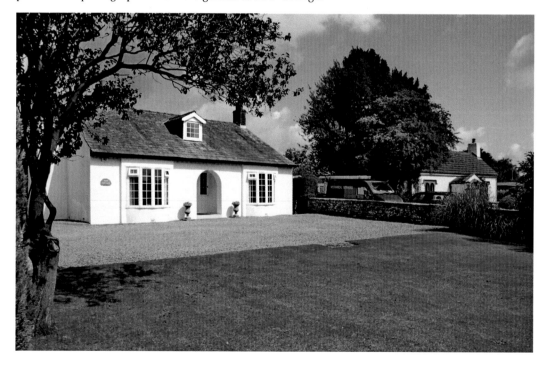

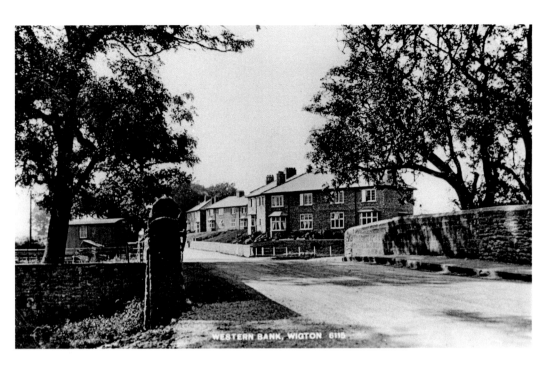

Western Bank

With victory in the First World War, returning soldiers were promised 'homes fit for heroes'. Wigton Urban District Council's contribution was a proposal to built 150 houses on Western Bank called Skiddaw View. By 1920 the first twelve properties with all the latest modern conveniences were finished, but there was only seven applications. Reluctance to leave town communities, no matter how poor the housing was, coupled with the higher rent on Skiddaw View resulted in the development being halted after just sixteen houses were completed. These views of Skiddaw View show little has changed over the years.

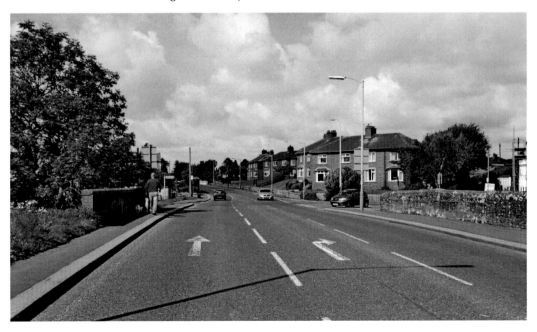

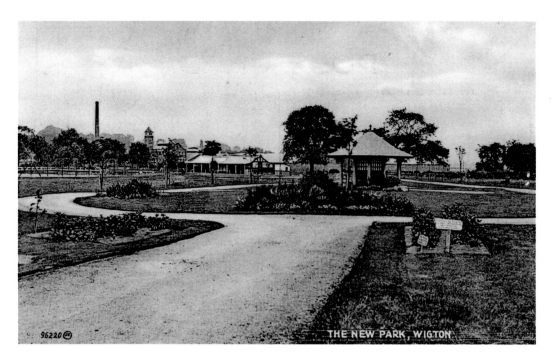

Wigton Park

The former jam factory's recreation grounds were purchased in 1923, for sports playing fields on Barton Laws and a public park near Western Bank. This 1930s picture shows the park with shelter, landscaped gardens and the Park Bowling Club pavilion and green (left of the shelter), established to relieve the over subscribed Throstle's Nest Bowling Club. In the background is the British New Wrap factory now Innovia Films. In 2009 the children's play area, right on the current picture was improved, whilst the bowling club is now masked by a beech hedge.

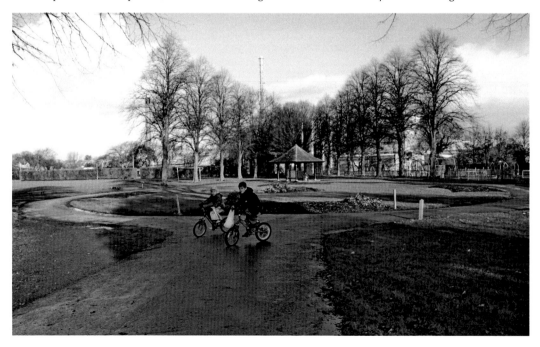

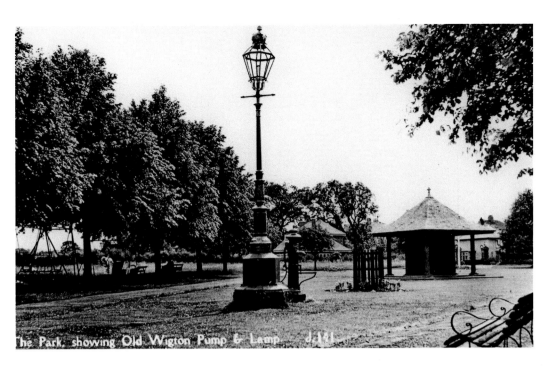

The Park, showing Old Wigton Pump & Lamp

Pump and Lamp in the Park

Before work started on the George Moore Memorial Fountain the pump and lamp were removed. The lamp was repositioned to light the Cornmarket and the pump sold as scrap. Rescued by John Hetherington landlord of the Half Moon Inn (now the site of the Library), it was erected in Highmoor Pinery as a decoration. With the opening of Wigton Park these two relics from Wigton's heritage were reunited in the park. Since then the pump and lamp (absent in the current image) have moved again and feature in the Water Street regeneration development.

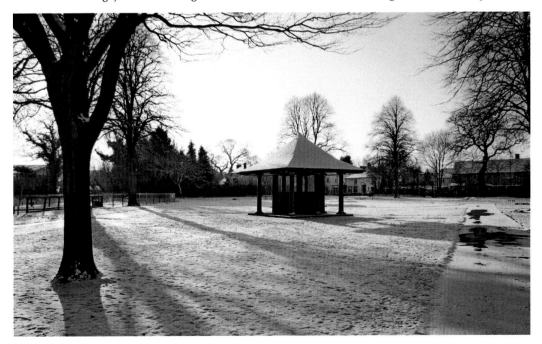

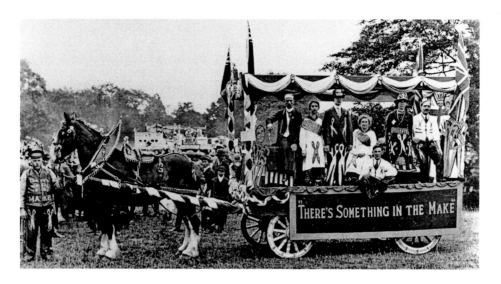

Carnival Fun

Redmayne's Carnival Float with rather solemn participants on board, advertise the tailor's art in their custom-made float and outfits. This photograph was taken at Highmoor Park before the procession down into Wigton, but recent Carnival processions have gathered at Kirkland before marching round the town and finishing on Barton Laws. The second picture from 2001 shows Wigton's own samba band the 'Allergaters' just after winning the Spirit of the Carnival Cup. Wigton Carnival is the highlight of the summer, involving the whole town, with hundreds of adults and children dressing up, creating floats and enjoying the party atmosphere as thousands of people pack the town.

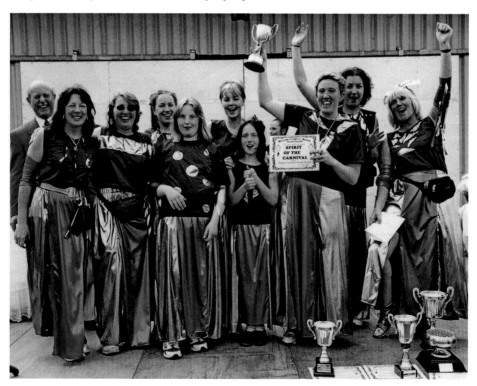

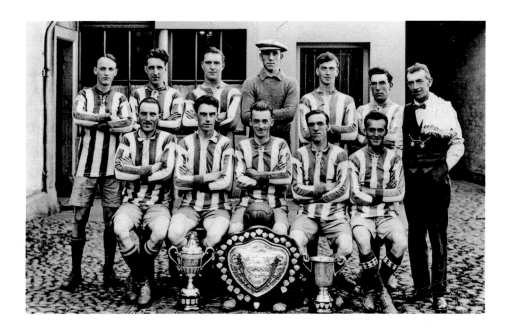

Wigton Football

Wigton Harriers AFC winners of the Carlisle & District League Division One, and the Carlisle Charity Shield and the Wigton Cowling Cup in 1925. Formed in 1889 the Harriers were just one of many Wigton football teams, which over the years has included the Rangers, Throstles, Juniors, Swifts, Wanderers and Athletic, together with numerous pub and factory sides. The Harriers still play, but there is a new team around, Abbeytown Ladies formed in 2008. Photographed here on Barton Laws the club is sponsored by R. Harrison & Sons (King Street butcher's) and compete in the Cumbria Womens' League, whilst also fielding under 10, 12, 14 and 16 junior teams.

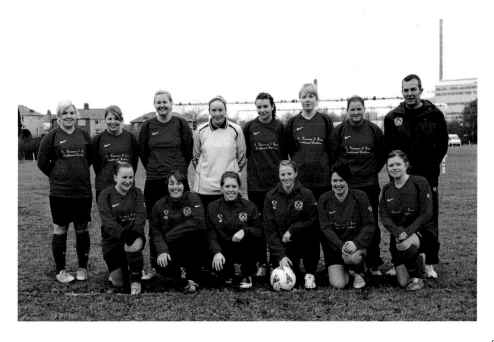

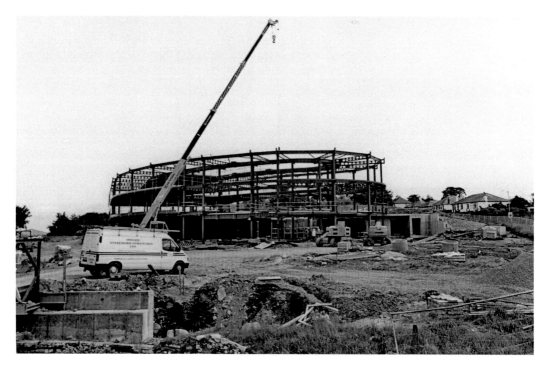

Innovia Films

Innovia Films, Research and Development building being erected on West Road in 2001, and the finished building in 2010. This building is concerned with film analysis and responsible for the creation of new films, many being biodegradable for use in labelling and food packaging, and others containing a polymer substrate to manufacture 'plastic' banknotes for Australia. The company continues to expand employing 1400 people worldwide and is by far Wigton's largest employer.

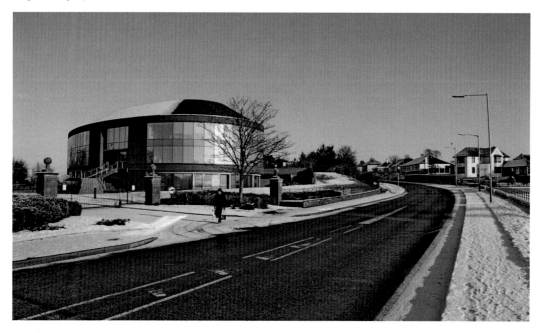

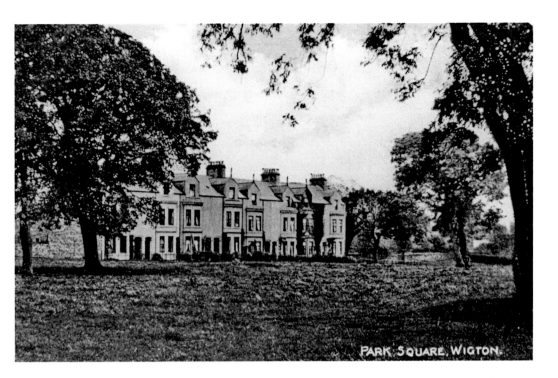

Park Square

In 1890 Robert Atkinson a West Street carpenter had a big idea. His dream was to build a square of town houses connecting West Street with George Street. Employing George Fell from Burnfoot (slater) and William McMillan of Union Street (builder) by July 1891 four houses were finished and three immediately sold as Wigton's newest suburb with its superior six-bedroomed properties took shape. Unfortunately only four further houses were built resulting in a terrace of houses and not a Square. Undeterred Robert still named his development Park Square, and went on to build South Terrace on Longthwaite Road. Today Park Square has hardly changed retaining its rural aspect.

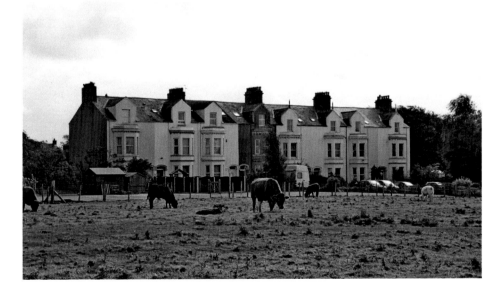

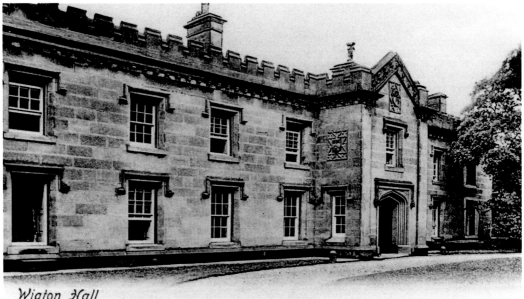

Wigton Hall

Wigton Hall

Probably dating from the fifteenth century, Wigton Hall is reputedly a clay dabbin which was enclosed in stone by the Reverend Richard Matthews who also added the Georgian windows, a porch and castellations, together with a private carriage drive from Wigton Hall to Longthwaite Road. Between 1866 to 1882 the Hall was John Bissell's Academy, a boys boarding school. Later it was rented out to several tenants, and then bought by British Rayophane in 1942. Today Wigton Hall is little changed on the outside, being used by Innovia Films as a luxurious hospitality residence.

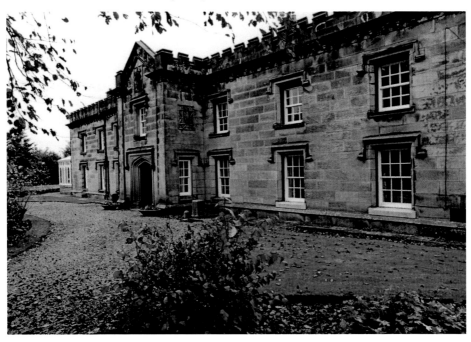

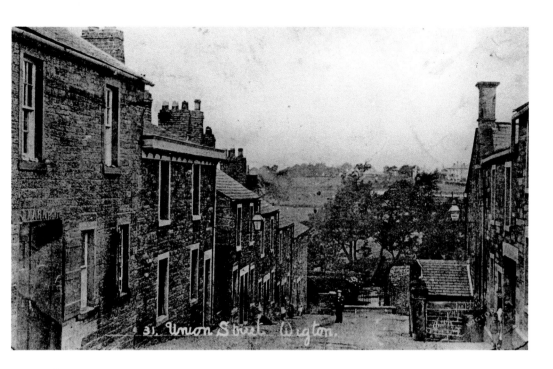

Union Street

1880s Union Street with its terraced sandstone cottages looking down hill towards the green fields and town houses of Station Hill. Above the left sided cottage door is inscribed 'J. Mark' marking the entrance to his brewery. Right is a fine gas lamp marked 'Oddfellows Hall' being the headquarters for the Wigton branch of the Oddfellows Society. Created in 1850 the Oddfellows were an early form of insurance company, with member's contributions paid to support ill colleagues off work, or to cover their funeral expenses. Today the hall is Arlosh Graphics studio, whilst the industrial complex of the Factory has blocked the view to Station Hill.

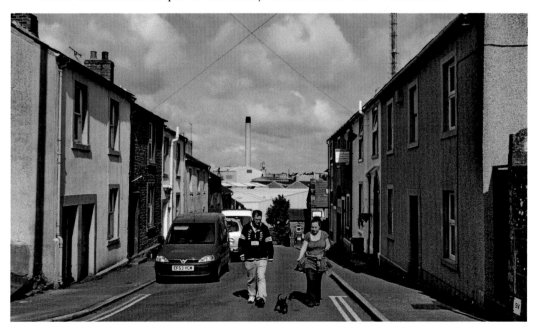

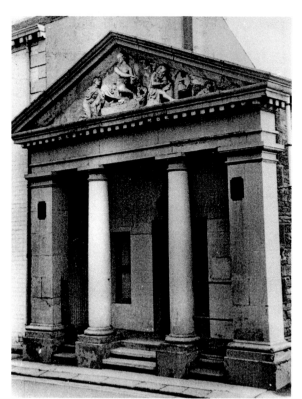

Mechanics' Institute

Imposing Tuscan columns, surmounted by a pediment and figures representing Wisdom receiving homage from Knowledge and Learning, carved by Wigton sculptor Irving Ray mark the entrance to Wigton Mechanics' Institute. Founded in 1851 to promote education among artisans for a small membership fee, the Institute benefited from book donations by Edwin Banks and held educational lectures. However membership was selective and a rival working mens reading room opened in Church Street with fees of 1*d* a week. In the 1970s the Institute was bought by the British Legion next door and the front removed. Recently the building has been converted into flats as the second picture shows, with the Hopes Estate Agent 'For Sale' sign hanging from the first floor.

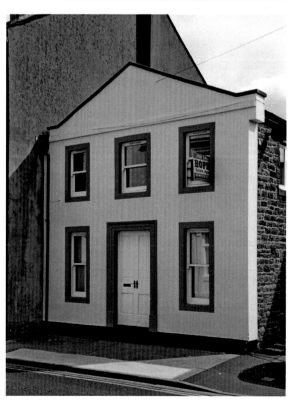